How to be the Parents of
HAPPY & OBEDIENT CHILDREN

How to be the Parents of
HAPPY & OBEDIENT CHILDREN

ROY LESSIN

Published by
Bible Voice, Inc. P.O. Box 7491
Van Nuys, California 91409

Scripture quotations in this publication are from the King James Version of the Bible.

Quoted portions in this book are used with permission of publishers or authors.

Published by Bible Voice, Inc.
P.O. Box 7491, Van Nuys, California 91409
Printed in U.S.A.

TO CHARLENE,
JOEY AND LYDIA —
My Special Gifts from God

Words of Appreciation

My deep heart appreciation to each one God has used to bless my life, and faithfully minister to me by providing the necessary help, encouragement and counsel needed to write this book.

"I thank my God upon every remembrance of you." Philippians 1:3

CONTENTS

INTRODUCTION

"Wherefore, by their fruits ye shall know them." Matthew
7:20

*"Even a child is known by his doings, whether his work be
pure, and whether it be right."* Proverbs 20:11

The purpose of this book is to help encourage parents to
arrive at the goal of having happy and obedient children.
These are the fruits God has promised for our children as we
follow His way. There are many teachings and philosophies
today dealing with the subject of how to raise children. I
believe a valid test of any teaching or philosophy on this
subject is to see what kind of fruit it is producing. If
happiness and obedience are not the end result, then
somewhere God's instructions have not been properly given
or applied.

The opportunity I had to observe my father-in-law farm
his crop, provided me with a helpful way of understanding
what steps I needed to take to see the fruits of happiness and
obedience produced in my children.

My father-in-law wanted his field to produce a good
crop. In order for this to happen, there were certain steps he
had to take. Just owning the field was not enough. If it was
neglected, it would only bring forth weeds and thistles. If the
field was going to produce a crop, it had to have seeds
planted in it. However, before seeds were planted, the soil
had to be prepared. The ground was turned over, weeds were
dug up and rocks removed. The soil was enriched with

nutrients and fertilizers. Thus, a successful harvest hinged greatly on the preparation of the soil before the seeds were planted.

After the seeds were in the ground, additional care was needed as the crop began to grow. The right balance of sunshine and rain would also determine the success of the crop.

I saw that God wanted to produce a successful crop in my children. He called it "the peaceable fruits of righteousness." They are the fruits of happiness and obedience. I knew this crop could not be produced automatically. God had given me, as a parent, certain responsibilities for soil preparation, seed planting and care of the crop as it developed. He would be faithful to provide the nourishment needed for that crop to be produced successfully.

I needed to help prepare the hearts of my children for the seed of God's Word through love and prayer. I needed to help pull the weeds that would develop in their character, and help encourage a bountiful harvest through my words and actions.

Sometimes people make the comment, "Training a child in God's ways is so much work!" It is true, it is work—hard work. But it is not an impossible task. A parent must always keep before him the purpose of his or her labor—the harvest.

When I first faced the responsibility of parenthood I was overwhelmed. I felt totally inadequate for the task. My prayer at the time was, "Lord, I've never been a parent before. I'm unskilled. What if I make mistakes?" Then the Lord's loving reply came as I read Psalm 32:8, "I will instruct thee and teach thee in the way which thou shalt go: I will guide thee with mine eye."

However, my uneasiness returned and again I prayed, "Lord, will my children really understand what I'm after? Will they see the things you want for them?" Again God answered, this time from Isaiah 54:13, "All thy children shall be taught of the Lord; and great shall be the peace of thy children."

Then I finally understood what God was saying. He was assuring me He understood my desire to train my children in His ways and see produced in them the fruits of happiness and obedience. He knew my weakness and assured me the responsibility of parenthood would not be a burden greater than I could bear, for He would be with me. He was showing me we were co-laborers together in the harvest field of my children's lives.

This book is written in two main parts. Part I is called "Parents." This section is not intended to be an in-depth study on the husband-and-wife relationship. (There are presently many fine books written on this subject.) Rather, the principles important to laying a proper foundation in the home that are vital to the successful training of happy and obedient children are covered.

Part II is called "The Training Box." This section covers the practical principles from God's Word that need to be applied to the lives of children as they are being trained by their parents. It is important to understand that there is no one chapter in this section that is the key to training happy and obedient children. The chapters must be taken as a whole. As you read you will discover one chapter works as a balance for the other.

There is one other point that is important to keep in mind as you read this book. Illustrations from my own family life and the lives of others that are used are meant only to illustrate a principle. The principle is the important thing for you to understand and apply in your family. Each family's needs are different. An illustration that shows what God did in my family does not mean He will do exactly the same thing in yours. God is creative and wants to show His love to you in His own special way. The relationship He has with you and your family will be unique. Allow Him to make

His own applications of the principles in His Word that He has given you and your family to follow.

Part I

PARENTS

GOD THE FATHER
↕
GOD THE SON
↕
GOD THE HOLY SPIRIT
↕
FATHER
↕
MOTHER
↕
CHILDREN

Note: When this illustration is used in the following chapters, an arrow going in an upward direction indicates submission, an arrow going in a downward direction indicates serving.

1

THE FAMILY AS GOD
INTENDED IT TO BE

"God created man in his own image . . . male and female created he them. And God blessed them, and God said unto them, Be fruitful, and multiply, and replenish the earth, and subdue it . . . and God saw everything that he had made, and, behold, it was very good." Genesis 1:27,28,31

The family is God's idea. He ordained it. He brought the first man and woman together in marriage. Their relationship was good. God blessed it. And it was a relationship intended to provide an atmosphere of love and leadership for the children who were to be the fruit of it.

But something happened to that first family. Adam and Eve chose to separate themselves from God. They chose to act independently. They overthrew the rule of God in their lives and in the life of the family. Then problems began. God never intended the family to function without Him. The rebellion of Adam and Eve against God was only the start of the tragedy and heartache that would come upon family life. Soon Cain, their son, murdered Abel, his brother. As the earth's population grew and mankind continued to live independently of God, adultery, perversion, permissiveness, and divorce became further enemies of the family.

Today, families everywhere are repeating the mistakes of the first family. The condition of rebellion that Isaiah described in the fifty-third chapter of his book still is true: "All we like sheep have gone astray; we have turned every one to his own way. . . ." Mankind as a whole has chosen to live apart from the rule and the blessing of God. The essence of sin is this rebellion chosen by the first family. And it continues to be chosen by individuals and by couples and by families to this day. The results are the same: many families are confused, frustrated, and without purpose. Selfishness has destroyed the family's foundation, leaving it unable to withstand the storms of our day that have come against it.

It must be made clear that it is not the institution of the family that is at fault. Rather, it is the way the family operates in our time that is the problem. Someone once said while viewing the great Mona Lisa of Leonardo da Vinci, "I can't see anything so special about that!" A museum guard standing nearby overheard the remark and replied, "Sir, it is not the Mona Lisa that is on trial." And so it is with the family. God instituted it. He ordained it. He blesses and protects it when it is properly maintained. It is not God's plan that is on trial. It is mankind which is on trial.

One day two men were building a house. About midway through the day they got into a heated argument. An hour passed and they were unable to settle their disagreement. Finally, in desperation, they called a passerby over to arbitrate their dispute.

"Tell me," said one carpenter, "when you're building a house, what goes up first, the walls or the roof?"

"Why, the walls, of course," replied the stranger.

"Hear that?" said the carpenter to his helper. "Start tearing down that roof!"

Now those fellows not only got mixed up about the order of building a house, but they left out the most important thing of all—the foundation. Jesus said, "Whosoever heareth these sayings of mine, and doeth them, I will liken him unto a wise man, which built his house upon a rock; and the rain descended, and the floods came, and the winds blew, and beat upon that house; and it fell not: for it was founded upon a rock" (Matthew 7:24,25).

As it is with building a house, so it is in building a family. A beautifully built house attracts attention. Its style and its furnishings reveal the personalities of both designer and owner. Yet hidden from the eye of the casual observer is the foundation of the house. That is hidden underground, unseen. Without it, the house itself would be worthless, and could not endure for long because rain and cold and heat and wind would reduce it to a shambles.

The building of an enduring family also requires a proper foundation. Paul states in 1 Corinthians 3:11, "For other foundation can no man lay than that is laid, which is Jesus Christ." God's plan is that every life and every family be built upon the foundation stone of Jesus Christ. To have Christ as the foundation means not only to believe in Him, but also to follow Him and to do what He says. To build the life of the family upon the foundation of Jesus Christ is to build upon a Rock—solid, stable, and unshifting.

Some people start out building their family upon the ideal of a perfect relationship with another person. They read some book or see a movie or hear a song that extols the joy of finding the perfect partner. They begin to believe that marriage and family depend upon finding the "right" partner. I once knew a man who read novels about the old American West. In the novels the hero always managed to find a perfect wife. She would love him, encourage him, cook his favorite food, keep the house looking perfect, and always say the loving word. The novels provided this man with an ideal. When he married he expected his wife to be the ideal woman that he had read about in the stories. It didn't take him long to find out that she wasn't the ideal woman he had read about. And he lived for years with the disappointment and resentment that his own ignorance created. And his family also suffered from his mistake.

Others try to build their family upon what I call "The Latest Article" approach. They pick up a magazine or a paper and discover a new article on marriage and the family. The tentative findings or conclusions of some psychologist or physician begin to form their opinions and convictions. But the magazine articles need to be weighed and tested by God's holy standards. The psychologists and physicians may tell us what *is*. God's Word tells us what *ought* to be. We must never make the mistake of letting an article or a lecture or statements by friends and relatives alter the true foundation for marriage. Christ is the true foundation. And it is Christ and His Word which should examine and judge what we read and hear and see.

The three main reasons for failure in a family are these:

First: a family that builds upon a philosophy of life that rejects Jesus Christ and His Word. Such a family will find itself to be like a ship set adrift on a stormy sea without a compass, a chart, or an anchor.

Second: a family that mixes the wisdom of the world with the wisdom of Christ. This results in a weak foundation that is part rock and part clay. It cannot withstand the pressures of a storm. A weak foundation produces a split in the superstructure. And Jesus said, "[A] . . . house divided against itself shall not stand" (Matthew 12:25).

Third: a family that tries to incorporate the standards and principles of God but leaves Him out. This creates an atmosphere that is legalistic, rigid, and unloving. Rules do not make a family. Love makes a family. And God is love.

The most important ingredient in a successful family is not *what* you bring into it, but *who* you bring into it. Its success does not rest upon what type of job you have, how happy you are at your work, what your bank account might be, or what neighborhood you live in. Many who have rewarding jobs, a fine income, and who live in plush neighborhoods still see their families fail.

It is only when Jesus is Lord in the life of the family that it can succeed. But He is not only the foundation upon which the family is built, He is its lifeblood, its heartbeat, its pulse. The successful family is not just churchgoing people, or good people, or pious people, but people in whom Jesus Christ is living. For it is His wisdom, His love, His strength, His life in their midst that allows a family to be all God intended it to be.

Jesus said, "Without me you can do nothing" (John 15:5). This saying applies to life in the family as well as every other aspect of a believer's life. To be a truly successful husband, wife, or parent in God's sight, you need Jesus. One does not have to begin as a perfect person with all answers to all questions when building a family upon God's firm foundation. But it is important to be dependent, to rely upon Christ's wisdom. A person wanting a successful family life must be open, teachable, and willing to say "Yes, Lord" when Christ shows His way or His wisdom in particular situations.

And above all it is important to remember that the family is God's creation. He ordained it. And He wants it to survive and function to His glory. As parents commit themselves and their families to Him, they will have the joy of discovering that God has also committed Himself to them. Together they will begin to experience the true meaning of family life.

2

WHOM TO GO TO FOR THE ANSWERS

"And ye shall know the truth, and the truth shall make you free." John 8:32

If you discover a problem with your refrigerator that you don't know how to fix, you will consult the manufacturer or a qualified repairman to fix it. If your plumbing goes bad you will call a plumber, not an electrician. A certain publishing company in California has a special paper-folding machine that was manufactured in Canada. The machine is of the best design and performance. Whenever the machine develops mechanical difficulties, the company does not contact a local repairman, who might know something about the average folding machine. Rather, it goes directly to the manufacturer in Canada. The manufacturer sends a specialist to repair the machine. The company knows that anyone not knowing how the machine was designed will not be able to repair it properly.

Problems and needs in families throughout the world today abound. And they are often complicated problems. Husbands and wives have difficulties in learning how to live together in harmony and love. Frustrated parents are unable to cope with their children. Some are even afraid of their children. A great search is going on to find the specialists who can repair the family. Yet many who call themselves "specialists" in family problems have no familiarity with the original *superior* design for the family given by God. Instead they understand only an *inferior* pattern—one that accepts divorce, infidelity, selfishness and rebellion as normal ingredients for the solution to marital and family problems.

If there is a problem in the family, the one to turn to for help is the one who designed the family. The family is God's idea. He designed it. He brought man and woman together in marriage. He told them to have children, to nurture them, and to provide for them. God gives to man and woman the guidelines they need to live together. He gives parents the instruction they need to raise happy and obedient children. God intends the home to be a place of joy and of blessing—a place that He can fill with His presence and joy. In 1 Chronicles 16:43 it is written, "And David returned to bless his house." The proper atmosphere of a household is created when it is the intention of each member to bless the other members. A main purpose of the Abrahamic Covenant was for God to bless His people and to make them a blessing to others. A Christian takes part in that special covenant of God with Abraham by faith. And as God's blessing is known to a Christian, God guides that Christian in practical steps to show His blessing extended into the family and out into the world.

In order to be a blessing in the family, a man must be the kind of husband and father God intends him to be. A woman to be a blessing must be the wife and mother God intends her to be. And children to be a blessing must be the brothers and sisters God intends them to be. To be what God intends is not difficult, unnatural, or superhuman. God's pattern does not require a special personality, a high mental aptitude or intellect. God's plan, in fact, lets each person in a family reach and realize the full potential of his or her own uniqueness. To be the kind of man or woman or child God intends requires only a responsible and obedient heart to Him. It means that each person takes the place God has given. Each can regard that position as a privileged position from which to serve Him and the others in the family. The crucial factor is surrender to God's way. In practical terms it means that choices and decisions are reached not through self-centered deliberations, but through a concern for others. God's kingdom is a kingdom of love. As people allow His rule to govern a home, love will be its main ingredient.

God's kingdom has a specific order to it. In the Trinity we see a relationship of harmony which comes from equality and submission. Within the Godhead there is unity and diversity. There is one God in three persons. The Father is God. The Son is God. And the Holy Spirit is God. They are not separate Gods but one God in three persons. From this mystery we learn the key to all successful relationships. In the Godhead there is absolute authority in the Father. The Son, although equal with the Father in His deity, is subject to Him. The Holy Spirit, although equal to the Father and the Son in His deity, is in subjection. When the Son left heaven and became a man to die on a cross as an atonement for sin, He did so in total obedience to the Father. His joy was in doing what the Father willed Him to do. After Jesus Christ was raised from the dead and ascended to the Father, the Father gave Him the gift of the Holy Spirit to minister to those who would follow Him. The Holy Spirit today delights to fulfill His special ministry of exalting the Son.

This authority and submission is extended into the family. Through the Holy Spirit the man of the home is to be in subjection to Christ. The wife, through the Holy Spirit, is to be in subjection to her husband. And the children are to be in subjection to their parents.

Each person is equal in importance before God and in the place God has for each person in the family. The intention is not for anyone to be considered inferior or superior, but for everyone to fit together in harmony and love.

The order of a family joined to God's order looks something like this:

God the Father

↑

God the Son

↑

God the Holy Spirit

↑

Husband/Father

↑

Wife/Mother

↑

Children

At first glance a child might think he is at the bottom of the ladder, getting the raw end of the deal by having all those people over him. A wife might have that feeling also, since her place is below the husband's. However, such feelings come from misunderstanding God's order. Actually, the lower down in the order you are the more blessed you are, for as you remember, the kingdom of God is a kingdom of love, not a kingdom of tyranny. The one in authority actually serves the others. As a person submits to the authority that God puts over him, the following takes place:

God the Father

↓

God the Son

↓

God the Holy Spirit

↓

Husband/Father

↓

Wife/Mother

↓

Children

In God's kingdom, submission doesn't put anyone in the position of being stepped upon. Rather, one is served. The children are in the most blessed place of all. The efforts and attention of those above are given for the safety, care and provision of those below. What a glorious position for a child—in subjection to those whose love and commitment are devoted to his own well-being and best interests!

God established the family at the time of creation. Both the fulfillment of the individual and the well-being of the family are a part of God's eternal purpose in creating the world. God's creation was not random, haphazard, or thoughtless. And we are not placed here to aimlessly drift through life lacking direction and purpose. God has a purpose for the individual and the family. As a part of God's purpose and design, the home and family are to be a place of unity and diversity, even as God's kingdom is a place of unity and diversity. This, however, depends upon each person being in a proper place of submission to God's authority in their lives.

A pastor counseling a husband and wife heard them confess that their home was in terrible condition. The wife said, "If my husband only loved me like he is supposed to our home would be in order."

The husband said, "If my wife would only submit to me like she is supposed to our home would be in order."

What is the problem here? The problem is that the man thinks that God is talking to him about the wife submitting. The woman thinks that God is talking to her about her husband loving. But when God says, "Wives, submit," He is talking to wives. When God says, "Husbands, love your wives," He is talking to husbands. God's order requires fulfillment of responsibilities. If that responsibility of a particular position is to love, that is what must be done, without worrying about someone else's responsibility. If it is to submit, that is to be done, without worrying about someone else's responsibilities. A person finds a new rest, assurance, and fulfillment doing what God commands in family relationships. As each family member asks the question, "God, what will you have me to do?" each one will discover God waiting and willing to answer.

3

FULFILLING THE PLACE
GOD HAS GIVEN A
WIFE AND MOTHER

"Wives, submit yourselves unto your own husbands, as unto the Lord."Ephesians 5:22

In order to raise happy and obedient children, each parent must understand the place and role God assigns. Below are several key principles concerning the wife's role of submission.

Submission Is a Privilege
The calling of a wife and mother is a high and a privileged calling. There is nothing negative or second class about it. God made woman different from man. Not inferior, just different. And when God brought a woman and a man together in marriage, He created a relationship of unity and oneness. He did not divide them up into a 50/50 arrangement, taking away half of the man and half of the woman to make a new and strange unit. In God's plan the man was to be 100 percent man and the woman 100 percent woman. Each was to fulfill a place in the family. Each one needed the other. Together they were one. Paul tells Titus to counsel women to "be sober, to love their husbands, to love their children, to be discreet, chaste, keepers at home, good,

obedient to their own husbands, that the word of God be not blasphemed" (Titus 2:4,5).

The woman gives the home its personality, creates its atmosphere, and sets its tone.

Submission Is Trust

Because the wife has such a strategic place in the family, God has taken certain responsibilities from her in order to free her to fulfill the needs and demands of that place. One way God frees a wife is by putting her in a place of submission to her husband. God takes from her shoulders the burden of making the final decisions that determine the direction the household will take. Putting a wife in the place of submission is putting her in the place of trust, not slavery. God puts the weight of leadership on the husband's shoulders and holds him responsible to look to Him for the proper decisions and directions. God wants the wife to trust Him *through* her husband. Through this principle God puts a wife under His special protective care, and frees her from the burden of inner striving, worry and anxiety. Often if a wife is filled with inner anxiety, it is because she has not entered into the place of trust and submission God wants her to have.

In 1 Peter 3, wives are encouraged to become daughters of Sarah. He says the key to doing this is to recognize the place Sarah gave Abraham in the family. The text says,

"Likewise, ye wives, be in subjection to your own husbands; that, if any obey not the word, they also may without the word be won by the conversation of the wives; while they behold your chaste conversation coupled with fear. Whose adorning let it not be that outward adorning of plaiting the hair, and of wearing of gold, or of putting on of apparel; but let it be the hidden man of the heart, in that which is not corruptible, even the ornament of a meek and quiet spirit, which is in the sight of God of great price. For after this manner in the old time the holy women also, who trusted in God, adorned themselves, being in subjection unto their own husbands: Even as Sarah obeyed Abraham, calling him lord: whose daughters ye are, as long as ye do well, and are not afraid with any amazement" (1 Peter 3:1-6).

When Sarah regarded her husband as lord she did so because of the place she saw God putting him in the family. She knew he was not "Lord" in the sense of being divine. Sarah knew Abraham's weaknesses and failures. She wasn't blind to his faults or needs. She didn't look upon him as lord because she pretended he had divine attributes. She looked upon him as lord because of the position he was given by God. God wanted her to trust Him through Abraham. The decisions Abraham made for the family would be God's. If she fought and rebelled against Abraham, God wanted her to see she was really fighting and rebelling against God.

This principle is illustrated in the account of Moses and Aaron's commission to go and free Israel from the oppression of Egypt. Before they were to address Pharaoh and the leaders of Israel, God gave Moses the following instruction: "He [Aaron] shall be thy spokesman unto the people: and he [Aaron] shall be, even he shall be to thee instead of a mouth, and thou shalt be to him [Aaron] instead of God" (Exodus 4:16). God was showing the high place of authority He puts upon someone who represents Him. As far as Aaron was concerned Moses was to be to him as God. Aaron knew that his brother was not God. He knew Moses' fears and failures. Yet because of the position God had placed Moses in, Aaron was to receive the words Moses spoke concerning Israel as the very words of God.

When the attitude behind submission is trust, the spirit and disposition of a wife will be one of love and confidence. She will not carry about a spirit of heaviness and unrest or resentment. Her joy will come from the inward peace of knowing God is in control of her life and her family. She will be strengthened with the constant joy of knowing she is pleasing the one who has called her to be a wife and mother.

Submission Establishes Authority

When a woman functions from a place of submission she puts herself in a tremendous place of strength. As she trusts God through her husband, it releases the power of God in her behalf. Instead of arguing with her husband or nagging him to be something or to do something, she can quietly trust God to be the one to cause her husband to see his needs. She soon can realize that God's way of getting her husband's attention is a lot more effective than her way.

When a woman takes a place of proper submission to her husband, she establishes her place of authority with the children. Authority is established when someone has another backing him. The policeman on the corner does not have the physical strength to stop a moving car, but he does have the authority to stop it. His authority comes from the fact that he has backing. Behind that outstretched hand are local, state and national governments. Here again is the back-up system for a wife:

God the Father
↓
God the Son
↓
God the Holy Spirit
↓
Husband/Father
↓
Wife/Mother
↓
Children

When a wife submits to her husband as unto the Lord,

she is not destroying or subverting her authority in the home, she is establishing it. When a woman tries to undermine her husband's position in order to become "boss" of the family, she is cutting off her own strength and weakening her position in the home. Children who know that their mother is being backed up by their father quickly respond to the order of things, and they begin to develop strength, stability, and confidence in their own lives.

Submission Is Not Silence

When a woman is in the place of submission, it does not mean that she becomes silent and merely waits for her husband's next directive. God has made the husband dependent upon his wife—she is his helpmeet. God has given her special insights into things, a certain intuition and a special ability to see matters from a protective point of view. A wife has a responsibility before God to share with her husband in a loving way how she feels and what she thinks. A man needs her viewpoint, her counsel, and her inspiration.

Men simply do not have the ability to "go it alone" in the family. A woman who does not share her insights with her husband does the family a disservice. But when a woman has openly shared her heart and mind with her husband, she must yield the burden of the final decision to him.

I discovered this same principle to be true both in the church and in business. For years I knew Jesus was my Lord, but I wouldn't allow Him to direct me through other members of the body of Christ. My response for years was "Jesus is my Lord, so don't tell me what to do. I get my orders directly from Him." One day God put me in a business relationship with some other Christian men and He used this time to teach me a very valuable lesson. He showed me that the principles of submission that apply to a wife toward her husband are the same principles that apply to a working relationship. I saw that on the job I had to trust God through the leadership He had placed over me. I also saw that the others needed me both for my skills and for my ideas.

Before I learned this principle, I used to go into our staff meetings with a lot of ideas about what the business should do. I would even preface certain suggestions with the statement, "God gave me this idea." But instead of getting an enthusiastic response, I got only blank stares and silence. In my resentment I would begin to push my ideas and try to make my associates accept them. And when they still rejected my ideas, I would leave them, feeling hurt and disappointed. I could not understand why they were unable to receive what I had believed to be God's inspired ideas.

Now in our business meetings when I have an idea, I still share it, even with enthusiasm. But after I've shared it, I leave it, confident that if it would prove to be the best thing for the company, God would endorse it by making His approval clear to everyone concerned.

If a wife feels her husband is about to make an unwise decision, she should share that with him in a loving way, not as his critic, but as his helpmeet. If he chooses to press ahead anyway, she ought not to challenge him; she should let the matter rest. And if the husband's decision produces a failure of some sort, she should not retaliate with "I told you so." Instead a wife should trust in God that He will use even the failure to teach the husband and the wife some valuable lesson. This attitude of trust is what Peter calls "the ornament of a meek and quiet spirit, which is in the sight of God of great price."

Submission Is Praise

The Bible states that a woman is to honor and praise her husband (see 1 Peter 3:2, Amplified Version). It is the attitude she carries toward her husband that greatly affects the success or failure of her submission and his ministry. True victory in submission is a matter of her heart *delighting* in it rather than just an outward conformity. "I delight to do thy will, O my God" (Psalm 40:8).

Some women seem to have taken up the special calling of doing all that they can to put down their husbands. They always make a point of telling others about their husbands' failures and faults. Most women would be in for a real surprise if they realized how few people really care to hear all the negative details of someone else's partner. In fact, if such negative talk does anything, it only puts the woman in a bad light. After all, who married this man she ridicules?

If, on the other hand, a woman believes that her husband is God's choice for her partner, then it is easy to honor, praise, and encourage him. She can believe that God knew exactly what she needed when He gave her her husband. This can be the case even if the man is not a Christian. God uses non-Christian husbands in wonderful ways to help women develop Christian character.

Submission Is Contentment

"But godliness with contentment is great gain. For we brought nothing into this world, and it is certain we can carry nothing out. And having food and raiment, let us be therewith content. But they that will be rich fall into temptation and a snare, and into many foolish and hurtful lusts, which drown men in destruction and perdition. For the love of money is the root of all evil: which while some coveted after, they have erred from the faith, and pierced themselves through with many sorrows. But thou, O man of God, flee these things; and follow after righteousness, godliness, faith, love, patience, meekness" (1 Timothy 6:6-11).

"He that is greedy of gain troubleth his own house;

but he that hateth gifts shall live" (Proverbs 15:27).

Submission to God's model for the family also means that a wife will submit to God's financial structure for the family. A leading cause for marital breakups in America is disagreement over finances. If a wife is discontented over financial matters, and if she continues to want more and more material possessions, the home cannot be a happy one. Books, magazines, movies, television, radio, and catalogues constantly tell people that they need more things in order to be happy. Women are a special target of advertising; and often the appeal is to pride, vanity, or greed. A discontented wife can put tremendous pressure on a man to work longer hours in order to earn more money in order to get the things that she desires. But a woman who is content in the financial structure God has given her family can know a new freedom and rest in her life. Following God's order also provides her with the assurance that it is His will to bless the home and to provide for the family. She also can experience the excitement that comes from waiting to see how God will provide for the family's needs.

On our anniversary one year, my wife wanted to buy me a surprise gift. At that time she didn't have any money she could call her own. She prayed and asked the Lord to directly send her some money without my knowing about it. Shortly after she prayed we were visiting a friend's church and after the meeting a man introduced himself to my wife. As he shook her hand, he left some money in her palm! It was a fresh example to her that the Lord knows her every need and cares about every detail of her life. "Delight thyself also in the Lord; and he shall give thee the desires of thine heart" (Psalm 37:4).

Submission Is Service

The main motivation for each member of the family is

to serve the others in love. Jesus taught, "He that is greatest among you shall be your servant" (Matthew 23:11). A wife serves her family by submitting to her husband. Submission is a spiritual service. It is an active force. It expresses itself in ways that will be for the highest good of those being served. A woman's service to her husband and family will especially express itself by simple encouragement. A wife's encouragement inspires her husband and her children and motivates them to strive to do the best they can in that which God has called them to do.

A very important way a wife serves her family also is through the service of prayer. Through prayer—the silent and least noticed work a wife can do—a wife lifts and strengthens those she serves.

A wife also serves in very practical ways, of course. A woman may be home alone much of the day, but the time alone need never be boring. Preparations for the homecoming of children from school and husband from work can take many forms. Even the smell of freshly baked cookies or bread tells a child that mother has taken a special way to show her love. The cleaned and straightened rooms give children and husband a feeling of order and calm after a busy, exhausting day. A wife's tone of voice can lift the spirit of one who is troubled by work or study. Through an attractive, orderly home, an atmosphere is set which can help conquer the gloom and disharmony of the world.

4

FULFILLING THE PLACE
GOD HAS GIVEN A
HUSBAND AND FATHER

"Husbands, love your wives, and be not bitter against them."
Colossians 3:19

*"Likewise, ye husbands, dwell with them according to
knowledge, giving honor unto the wife, as unto the weaker
vessel, and as being heirs together of the grace of life; that
your prayers be not hindered." (1 Peter 3:7)*

Leadership Is Submission

In God's order, the man is put in a position of leadership for the family. Often a man can misunderstand
this role. He might think that God has made him "The
Big Boss," and that his wife must submit to him under
God as he gives commands. This attitude will often be
accompanied by anger, frustration and resentment. Once
again we need to refer to our diagram of God's order for the
family in order to see the complete picture of relationships
in the family.

God the Father

↑

God the Son

↑

God the Holy Spirit

↑

Husband/Father

↑

Wife/Mother

↑

Children

It is true that God placed the man in the position of leadership for his family. A wife is to be in subjection to her husband. But, what a man must realize is that the wife is not the only one who is called to a place of submission. Just as the wife is under the husband, and in subjection to him, so the husband is under Christ and is in subjection to Him. A man does not escape the principles and responsibilities of submission because he is the leader of his family. A man must submit to Christ in the same manner as he expects his wife to submit to him.

Many homes stumble along in confusion and disorder simply because the husband demands submission from his wife, but fails to fully submit himself to his Head, Christ. Such a failure can make it difficult for a wife to properly submit to her husband, because she lacks a clear example of submission from her spouse. It is the husband's responsibility as leader to gently lead and teach the way of submission through his own example. If the husband is out of order in his relationship to Christ, it is to be expected that a wife has no clear example to follow.

A common course a husband so often may follow, when he does not take his proper place of leadership in the home, is to push off upon his wife the responsibility of leadership that he should be fulfilling. Because he frustrates God's order in his own life, he soon senses his inadequacy for leadership. But, instead of turning in his failure to Christ for help, he retreats and surrenders his position to his wife. He puts a load on her God never intended her to carry. To complicate matters, many women accept the role of leadership, instead of keeping their hands off and allowing God to continue to deal with their husbands. They take the leadership for fear the family will not hold together. When this happens, many husbands sink into total withdrawal, thinking that since their wives took over the responsibility it must be right. But if a husband follows Christ's leadership, he finds himself free from worries that may accompany leadership.

If a husband finds his place under Christ, he will experience the peace, the confidence, and the courage to lead even in difficult times. Submitted to Christ, he will find Him to be his complete sufficiency for leadership. When his family has needs, he will find Christ is his Provider. When his family has problems, he will find Christ is his Burden Bearer. When his family needs direction, he will find Christ is his Shepherd.

Leadership Is Serving

"Husbands, love your wives, even as Christ also loved the church, and gave himself for it" (Ephesians 5:25).

"For the husband is the head of the wife, even as Christ is the head of the church: and he is the saviour of the body" (Ephesians 5:23).

Someone once said, "The greatest thing a father can do for his children is love their mother." A husband is not only commanded by God to love his wife, but to love her as Christ loved the church. This is the highest example of love to follow. Christ expressed His love for the church by giving Himself for it. A husband who loves his wife this way gives of himself. There is no holding back, and no reservation. The main concern is for the highest good of his wife and family.

As a man places himself under the authority of Christ in his family, he will begin to manifest the mind and nature of Christ to every family member. A man will find himself in the position of a servant before his family. Christ, the Head of the church, does not lead it as a tyrant; He tenderly cares for the church. Even so, the man God places in leadership over a family serves in the same manner.

There are two important ways in which a man serves his family. One is by giving the family the leadership it needs. The captain of a ship does not turn the wheel over to his passengers. He is aware of the long journey and the storms the ship may encounter. Because it is his duty to assure that both ship and passengers arrive safely at the desired destination, he does not abandon his ship. He does not for a moment think the passengers can get along without him. In the same way for each family member to arrive at the place God has prepared, they need leadership. As a man lovingly serves his family through his leadership, family members will learn that the decisions and directives he brings are not for his own ends but for the good and best of all.

Another way a man serves his family is by providing for them. Many men limit this to mean just providing material goods for their families. They feel that if they work their 40 hours, pay the bills, feed and clothe everyone, and from time to time take everyone out for something special to do, or dine, their obligation is fulfilled. Of course, providing the material needs of a family is an important service. But it is not the only aspect of providing.

A group of women once were asked what they thought to be their area of personal need best met by their husbands. These women confessed that spiritual needs were most important. Husbands have a special capacity for providing those needs such as spiritual counsel, direction, prayer, encouragement and instruction. The husband in God's order has not only the position but the spiritual capacity through Christ to meet these needs. This is part of the priestly ministry of the husband: he stands between God—the source of all love and concern—and mediates or carries that love through himself to his wife and children.

A man's family is his most important place of spiritual ministry. It should never be considered secondary to some outside work or concern. In 1 Timothy 3:5 and Titus 1:5,6 it says that before a man can be considered for ministry within the church, he must first be a faithful minister at home.

The relationship between home life and spiritual calling is a close one. And our sensitivities and responsibilities can intersect in surprising ways. Once I was taking a missionary to the airport to board a plane for Europe. On the way God prompted me to give the person the ten dollars I had in my wallet. Since it was all the money I had at the time, I resisted the prompting of God, rationalizing that my own need was too great to give it away. The missionary left, and I returned home with my ten dollars in my pocket. When I arrived home, I discovered that my young son had suddenly become sick while I was away. Rushed to a doctor, he received treatment and recovered. The emergency medical treatment cost exactly ten dollars.

I learned a valuable lesson concerning obedience to God's prompting for practical service. But I also came to understand that my role as a father and provider is tied in a relation of interdependence to a spiritual ministry. To act in disobedience in one area brings weakness and vulnerability to an other. My disobedience in ministry opened my family to unexpected attack.

God has given the husband special grace to be a type of spiritual shock absorber for his family. A shock absorber on a car is designed to cushion the impact of the bumps and rough places a car goes over while riding the highway. As the shock absorber does its job it smooths the ride for the passengers. In a similar way, as a man takes the place of leadership for his family, he is out ahead, cushioning the rough places of his family's journey. He provides a front line of defense against the enemies that would try to destroy the harmony of family life.

Whenever a husband falters in leadership it is important that every family member uphold him in prayer. Once when Israel was in a great battle, they depended on the upraised hands of Moses to gain the victory they needed. When Moses tired, he depended on those next to him to put their hands under his to keep his arms upraised. It is the same in any family. No one is really meant to stand alone. But every member is dependent upon every other family member.

5

SERVING TOGETHER

"Can two walk together, except they be agreed?" Amos 3:3

In the Bible God speaks many times of His role as a Father to His people. The relationship God holds with parents too is a relationship of a father to his children. By this relationship God teaches a husband and wife what parenthood means. Parents can learn something of how to raise their children by closely observing their relationship to God. If, however, a husband's or a wife's relationship to God is not what it ought to be, then they can expect the family to falter. Because a mother or father has not learned to be a proper son or daughter of God, they will lack the wisdom needed to raise happy and obedient sons and daughters of their own.

Because some parents fail to obey God as they should, they seek out other ways to effectively raise their children. Some go to various methods that are contrary to the principles of parenthood that God gives in His Word. "Beware lest any man spoil you through philosophy and vain deceit, after the tradition of men, after the rudiments of the world, and not after Christ. For in him dwelleth all the fulness of the Godhead bodily" (Colossians 2:8,9). Others make efforts to become pals with their children, even to the point of dressing like them, and acting like them. Although friendship with children is certainly a part of parenthood, to become a child's "best buddy" falls far short of what is needed in a parent-child relationship. Children need mothers and fathers who respond to them with the same leadership and loving care that God shows to His children. From the example of parents, children learn at a young age to honor and to trust in God.

Parents as a Unit

I once saw a cartoon in which two donkeys tied to opposite ends of a long rope pulled and tugged against one another as they tried to reach stacks of hay lying at opposite ends of a field. Each stubbornly struggled to go its own direction, thinking only of the good food within sight. But the rope was not long enough for each to eat at its own stack, so neither of them could eat. Finally, the donkeys discovered that if they went to a haystack *together*, they could each fulfill their objective and eat all the hay they desired.

Too many homes are torn by the same sort of disunity as the donkeys first exhibited. Tied together by marriage bonds, husband and wife try to go their separate ways to seek fulfillment. But for real fulfillment a husband and wife need one another. God joined them to be a unit. When they come together in agreement with a singleness of mind and purpose, their goals as a family unit can be reached.

The experience of a fundamental unity of purpose in raising a family is more important than any technique or formula for keeping a happy family. Happy and obedient children are not the result of parents who have applied a special technique, but are the results of parents who have first established a right relationship with God and each other and together from that relationship obediently respond to the direction God gives them. Parents must guard against the temptation to act independently. Independent action or decision threatens the unity of the home. Without this unity the same confusion and competition exist as when two artists try to paint different pictures on the same canvas.

It is a regrettable development that so many families find that the only way tensions in the home can be relieved is to let each member break loose and wander independently toward some private goal. Such a development in family life is not a sign of maturity, but a sign of deterioration of family life. It means that God's standards have been abandoned. And each member is set adrift to do that which is right in his own eyes.

The immediate result of parents set adrift to go their own ways is that children have no sense of direction or authority. After all, God instructs children to obey their parents in all things. "Children, obey your parents in all things: for this is well pleasing unto the Lord" (Colossians 3:20). He does not say to obey only one parent. Both parents are to be obeyed. Children have the right to know what to obey and what is expected of them. This is impossible if parents are not in unity. And to achieve unity parents must spend sufficient time together sharing and discussing what is and what is not acceptable behavior for their children. They need to agree specifically on what "yes" means and what "no" means in the context of the home; and they must guard against letting children split them on an issue.

Children quickly discover how to play one parent against another if there isn't unity within the home. If a parent is not sure what the other would say or do regarding an important decision in the home, he or she should withhold any definite word from the children until he or she has had an opportunity to discuss the matter privately with the other parent. It is more important to wait and guard unity than to risk disunity. Of course, if husband and wife disagree after discussing a matter, a wife should submit and leave the responsibility for decision to the husband. And when a husband is doubtful about how to decide, he should carefully consider his wife's viewpoint.

But once a husband and wife have discussed a family issue and are in a place of unity, either by having similar viewpoints or through the wife's submission when they differ, the task of communication to the children is a simple one. Parents will not openly challenge one another. And there is no ground upon which the children can be confused, since they will see that mother and father are united.

When a husband is away from home a wife must handle problems with the children alone. But she can act with confidence and strength because she knows her husband's mind (if they have had proper discussion). She can simply do exactly what her husband would do if he were home. A woman's authority is established in this way. She should never have to fear her own children.

Women who allow their children to do things in their husbands' absence that they would never do in the husbands' presence actually threaten their own authority and bring frustration and tension to themselves and to their children. It must be remembered the authority for parenthood comes from God. It is His order that is being maintained by proper relationships within the family. Unity in parenting is crucial to that order.

6

RESULTS

"Let us not be weary in well doing: for in due season we shall reap, if we faint not." Galatians 6:9

A parent would like a son or daughter to obey happily whenever asked to do something. Yet many parents rarely have happy obedience from their children. Parents would be willing to settle simply for obedience. Happy obedience they have come to believe is too much to expect.

A scene all too familiar when out shopping today is this one: a mother and her child are arguing in front of the candy display in a supermarket.

"I want some candy," Johnny says.

"No, honey, no candy today," says mother.

"Why?" says Johnny.

"You've had enough candy this week."

"But I want some of this candy," replies Johnny.

"No, Johnny, now come along!" says mother.

"I want some of this candy!" yells Johnny.

"I said no! Now come along or I'll have to spank," says mother, nervously looking about to see if anyone has heard her threat.

"Candy! Candy!"

"Shut up!"

"Waaa! Waaa!"

"Shut up!"

"Waaa! Waaa!"

"Okay. Here's your candy, now come on!"

Johnny learned at an early age that if he gets loud and stubborn in public places, mother gets embarrassed quickly and gives in to his demands. Johnny has won another victory in the battle of his will against his parents.

Not every parent reacts in the same way to stubbornness. So some children use other techniques to get the same result—their own way—some whine and pout, while others talk baby-talk, cuddle up, or bat their eyes. Some throw tantrums and roll on the floor. Some hold their breath until their parents panic. But in so many cases that we all have observed the result is the same. Parents give in to the demands of the children.

Another familiar scene is when a parent or grandparent has finished shopping and is ready to leave the store; but the child decides to stay.

"Okay, Janie, it's time to go," says mother or dad or grandpa.

"No, I want to stay and look at some more things."

"It's time to go home now."

"No, let's stay!"

"Okay, if you don't come now, I'll have to leave without you. Good-bye, Janie."

The threat to leave without the child seems to make the parent think that the child will want to join him or her. Children like Janie know that the parent does not intend to leave them. So, if Janie holds out, she knows that mommy or daddy will come back into the store for her.

The image of the disagreeable, disgruntled, and disobedient child is so common that it is a familiar cliche in films and television shows. In fact, the obstreperous child is so much a part of American entertainment that for years I thought disobedience and stubbornness were expected characteristics of all children.

An old movie brings to mind a particularly vivid scene. There is the father sitting at the breakfast table trying to feed several children. One is a toddler who sits in a highchair. The father does his best to get that child to eat his oatmeal. He pleads, he begs, but no amount of coaxing can interest the child in eating. Instead, the child ends the whole scene by not only winning the battle of refusing to eat his oatmeal, but also by emptying the entire bowl over his father's head. The scene is funny on the screen. But it is sad when seen in reality.

A problem many parents face today is that they've seen and heard many negative impressions of parenthood. Because of this they don't expect to see the results of happiness and obedience in their children, even though they desire it.

An important step for parents is to raise their level of expectation to the point where they are shocked and disappointed to see disobedience in their own children. Surely it is not God's will that parents should settle for anything less. It took many years for me to finally come to the place where I could believe God had answers for my questions about how to be a parent to happy and obedient children. By the time our first child was born I was convinced that God's Word held the answers for successful parenting. But, it was not until our second child was born that I realized how much God's principles had influenced our family life.

One evening we visited some friends for dinner. After dinner the children all ran off to play, and we parents visited in the living room. Soon it was time to leave, so I called out, "Children, it's time to go."

"Okay, Daddy," came the reply. And within a few seconds both children were in the living room ready with their jackets to put on.

"Did you see that?" my friend exclaimed to his wife.

"Yes, I did. That's amazing!" she said.

"What's amazing?" I asked.

"Your kids," my friend said. "When you said that it was time to go, they obeyed you without any fuss."

What my friends saw to be amazing I had come to expect, since for some time my wife and I had been training our children according to principles we had found in the Bible. It did not seem unusual for our children to obey us. We expected that as normal behavior!

But obedience and happiness for children does not come automatically. No one ever has to teach a child to disobey; disobedience seems to come naturally. Selfishness and rebellion and a desire to have one's own way show themselves in children at a very young age. Yet these marks of sinfulness and depravity are the very things that Scripture proclaims can be overcome. That is the Good News of the Bible. And that means that children do not have to be a burden, a grief and a frustration to their parents. They can be a joy, a blessing, and a fulfillment of their parents' highest hopes.

God did not intend parenthood to be a huge burden. Rather, parenting is a great privilege. "Children are a heritage of the Lord," says Psalm 127:3. God wants parents to have the same attitude toward their children that He has toward His spiritual children. "The Lord thy God in the midst of thee is mighty; he will save, he will rejoice over thee with joy; he will rest in his love, he will joy over thee with singing" (Zephaniah 3:17).

God does not begrudge His children, but joys over them and welcomes His responsibility to train them. He doesn't neglect them. It gladdens Him to be called their Father.

A positive attitude toward parenthood is expressed through a dedication to God of children by parents. Through this dedication a parent says, "I welcome my calling as a parent, and I look to God for His strength and wisdom so that I might raise my child in a way pleasing to Him." A dedication also acknowledges God's love for children. And it gives parents an opportunity to confess that they desire their children to serve God with their lives. In 1 Samuel it is written of Hannah, "For this child I prayed; and the Lord hath given me my petition which I asked of him: therefore also I have lent Him to the Lord; as long as he liveth he shall be lent to the lord" (1:17).

A husband and wife must never forget that God has chosen *them* to be parents for their children. That means that they cannot expect the school or the church or a baby-sitter to be parents. Parents must guard against the temptation to pass the responsibility of parenthood to someone else. And it is only with the acceptance of responsibility of parenthood that parents can experience the true excitement and adventure that loving, guiding, teaching, and nurturing children can bring. They can discover how God teaches them through each new growing phase their children enter. They can discover the wisdom God gives in the face of situations they never faced before. A parent of a one-year-old does not need to know how to guide and direct a fifteen-year-old child. Part of the excitement of parenting is the coming to wisdom as the child grows. As parents obey God day by day in what He shows them, that obedience will become their preparation for tomorrow.

God has not intended for parents to learn how to train their children by a trial and error system. People do not have to find wisdom in parenting only after the children have grown up and left the home. Every parent who chooses to obey God can believe Him for the wisdom they need each day as they seek to raise happy and obedient children.

Part II

THE TRAINING BOX

LOVE

EXAMPLE

"Train up a child in the way he should go: and when he is old, he will not depart from it."

Proverbs 22:6

DISCIPLINE

TEACHING

7

THE TRAINING BOX

LOVE

| EXAMPLE | "Train up a child in the way he should go: and when he is old, he will not depart from it."
Proverbs 22:6 | DISCIPLINE |

TEACHING

Proverbs 22:6 tells us that as parents we have a responsibility to train up our children in the way they should go. This particular text does not tell us how we are to do that. Therefore, I have put lines around the text to box in the basic principle. Then I will show how the Bible in other places teaches how to fulfill this principle.

To bring up children in the way God directs, we need to give attention to more than one thing. Love and discipline, teaching and example, all working together, bring about the training our children need. To fit these elements together provides a framework for training happy and obedient children.

Sometimes happiness and obedience are not seen because one side of the box has been pushed to such an extreme that it becomes out of balance with the rest. For example, some parents emphasize love to the point that they ignore discipline completely. Others push discipline to the point that they regard anyone who talks of love to be soft in their views. It is important to see every side of the box as vitally important. We cannot afford to ignore one side and indulge the other. Balance is so important to children's training.

Love without discipline produces spoiled children. Discipline without love produces discouragement and a broken spirit in children. Teaching without example produces bitterness and resentment. Example without teaching produces unstable and insecure children. Lacking any one of the absolutes of God's Word, distorts their growth. They need to build their lives on God's firm, solid and unshifting foundation.

These problems are serious ones when we see the damaging results they can bring to children. One result is that they can wander as aimless idealists or bitter rebels through life—easy prey for every radical ideology that happens along. Proper teaching provides a foundation of certitude built upon God's Word.

In the next few chapters we will look at each side of the training box to discover from scripture what it means to train children in love, discipline, teaching and example.

There is also a special promise for parents in Proverbs 22:6. It says if we train our children in the way they should go, they will not depart from it. That promise is included to be an encouragement to every parent who sets out to bring up a child in God's ways. Once I thought that promise meant something different from what it actually says. I thought it meant "when he is old he will return to the way you have trained him." That is, if a parent trains a child in God's ways when he is young—taking him to church, giving him Bible verses to memorize, etc.—then after a teenage period of rebellion, he would return, like the prodigal son, and claim his spiritual heritage.

I know that my earlier understanding of the verse accurately describes what has happened in many cases. And we must not discount the work of God done in adult lives who have departed from their early years of Christian training. But we should not accept this as being the way God has intended things to be. It is to turn the prodigal son into a normal example. We must raise our expectations much higher than that. We must make them conform to exactly what is promised in Proverbs 22:6. "Train up a child in the way he should go: and when he is old, he *will not depart from it.*"

If a person is on a journey, and suddenly leaves the trail and goes in a direction other than his destination, he has *departed* from the way. Later, if he gets back on the trail and once again heads toward his destination, he has *returned* to the way. On the other hand, if a person is on a journey and stays on the trail until he reaches his destination, he has *not departed* from the way. "Not departing" is the promise of this verse.

Children can be a blessing to parents. Parents don't have to wait in fear for that anticipated teenage rebellion. God does not will that any person go through a period of rebellion. His desire is for a person, at every age of his life, to be a blessing to Him and others. Rebellion is surely not a normal part of development in the original plan of God. Everywhere in Scripture when people rebel, God treats it as sin. Yet people have so often accepted rebellion as normal.

An example of perfect sonship is seen in Jesus. Everywhere in the Bible we are encouraged to look upon Jesus as the one who lived a life pleasing to God and the one who is to be our example. When Jesus was baptized by John the Baptist, the voice of God was heard to say: "This is my beloved Son, in whom I am well pleased" (Matthew 3:17). God was pleased with His life, with the way He had lived those previous 30 years. What was Jesus doing in those years? He was living at home, being *in subjection* to His parents. He was a blessing to them and to His Father in heaven.

The Bible does speak of prodigal sons who leave home in rebellion and one day return. And parents should welcome home the wayward child with open and loving arms. But we miss the point of the Scriptures if we make the prodigal son an example of everyday Christian family experience.

One reason for our low expectations concerning children may be that we ourselves did not have happy and obedient childhoods. We may have been happy at times. But if we recall those times of happiness, we would have to conclude that often they were not obedient times of happiness. That is, we were happy because we were getting our own way or serving ourselves. That sort of happiness, of course, is not true biblical CHRISTIAN happiness. It is selfishness!

Let me say again: GOD WANTS YOUR CHILDREN TO BE HAPPY. Happy children is in God's order. Happiness is another word for being blessed with God's favor. God wants each person to know His blessing. His blessing brings joy, no matter what the outward circumstances may be. But also, GOD WANTS YOUR CHILDREN TO OBEY. Obedient children is in God's order. These two things are so closely linked that they are like the two sides of a coin. Each side may look different, but you must have both to have a genuine coin. Anything else is counterfeit.

Rebellion in children should *not* be our expectation.

Rather, loving, loyal, obedient children should be our expectation. And such children are what God expects as the experience of the normal Christian family.

8

LOVE

LOVE

Example	"He that loveth not, knowoth not God; for God is love." 1 John 4:8	Discipline

Teaching

Love is the basis of family life. It is the bedrock upon which the family is built. Without love as a foundation, all the techniques and skills in family living will fail. Another way to put it is that love is to a family what oil is to an engine. Without it, relationships grind and wear and eventually either malfunction or disintegrate. Without the warmth of love, family relationships become cold and hard and rigid. Love makes the difference between a happy family and a dictionary definition of a family.

There are two main expressions of love that children need. The first is the natural love of a parent. It is the kind of love that says "I welcome and accept my child into my family." It is the kind of love a child should get from the beginning. Even while the child is forming within the mother's womb this spontaneous and natural love can be expressed.

Unfortunately there are some parents who do not have this early experience of love for their yet unborn child because of selfishness or wrong thinking. Some think a child will interrupt their plans and ambitions and tie them down. Others think that parenthood is a burden and responsibility that they cannot accept. As a result, their children are treated as intruders into the family and are either rejected or resented.

A child needs to be loved and welcomed by its parents at its very conception because that is the moment God loves and welcomes a child. The psalmist explains God's deep and intimate involvement with children before their birth.

"O Lord, thou hast searched me, and known me. Thou knowest my downsitting and mine uprising; thou understandest my thought afar off. Thou compassest my path and my lying down, and art acquainted with all my ways. For there is not a word in my tongue, but, lo, O Lord, thou knowest it altogether. Thou hast beset me behind and before, and laid thine hand upon me. Such knowledge is too wonderful for me; it is high, I cannot attain unto it. Whither shall I go from thy Spirit? or whither shall I flee from thy presence? If I ascend up into heaven, thou art there: if I make my bed in hell, behold, thou art there. If I take the wings of the morning, and dwell in the uttermost parts of the sea; even there shall thy hand lead me, and thy right hand shall hold me. If I say, Surely the darkness shall cover me; even the night shall be light about me. Yea, the darkness hideth not from thee; but the night shineth as the day: the darkness and the light are both alike to thee. For thou hast possessed my reins: thou hast covered me in my mother's womb. I will praise thee; for I am fearfully and wonderfully made: marvelous are thy works; and that my soul knoweth right well. My substance was not hid from thee when I was made in secret, and curiously wrought in the lowest parts of the earth. Thine eyes did see my substance, yet being unperfect; and in thy book all my members were written, which in continuance were fashioned, when as yet there was none of them. How precious also are thy thoughts unto me, O God! how great is the sum of them! If I should count them, they are more in number than the sand: when I awake, I am still with thee" (Psalms 139:1-18).

God doesn't wait until a child is born before He becomes involved with that life. In the same way parental love is the love that says "Yes! I accept you, yes, I will nurture and provide for you." Parental love receives a child with joy and thankfulness, and acknowledges that young life as God's gift.

The second expression of love children need from their parents is that of Divine love. Natural, or parental love, is not enough. It has its limitations. Natural love expresses the parents' best interests. But Divine love expresses God's interests. Divine love is vital in enabling parents to have happy and obedient children. The Bible tells us, "The love of God is shed abroad in our hearts by the Holy [Spirit] which is given unto us" (Romans 5:5). A personal relationship to Jesus Christ is an experience of Divine love. And that experience of love can be expressed to any child in several ways.

It Is a Love that Wants the Best for a Child

Because God is love He desires the highest and best for all of His creation. God commanded Israel to love Him with all their heart, soul, mind and strength. He did not give this commandment out of selfishness. He gave this commandment out of love. Looking through all creation, He knew that there is nothing higher or better to be known than Himself. To love anything or someone more than God is to settle for second best. Parents loving their children with God's love will hold to this same standard. They will recognize that their children's personal relationship with God and the formation of His character within them is the best and highest goal they can have as parents.

Divine love expressed through parents will put maximum attention and concern upon a child's spiritual needs. But even when it comes to temporal needs, because love desires the best, it will be selective or discriminating. In other words, to desire the best means to recognize and reject some things as less than best. Divine love is not indiscriminate. God keeps His people *from* some things in order to give them other things that are better.

Therefore a loving parent keeps a child away from some things (or some things away from a child) because the parent wants the best. So it must be remembered that love has two sides. It desires the best. But to desire the best it must reject the less than best. Love says "no" as well as "yes."

It Is a Love from the Will

God loves us because He is love. Love is not something God only has or feels, He *is* love. His love means He wills the best and highest good. His love is constant and unchanging. The extension of this love to mankind is not controlled by any selfish emotion or mood. God does not love us only if we function properly. The Bible tells us, "We love him, because he first loved us" (1 John 4:19). While we were yet in our sins God loved us. God's love reaches out seeking to correct and restore, even if in rebellion a person rejects that love.

God's love through parents will touch children in the same way. Divine love will flow from the heart and will, keeping a parent from being ruled by selfish emotions or moods. It will provide proper motivation for parents to desire only the highest good and the best for their children. And it will also keep parents from manifesting an attitude of rejection toward their children if they falter or rebel. It will always seek ways to correct and restore. Divine love never gives up.

It Is a Love that Gives

"For God so loved the world, *that he gave* his only begotten Son, that whosoever believeth in him should not perish, but have everlasting life" (John 3:16).

Divine love is a giving, sacrificing love. Divine love in parents is also a giving and sacrificing love. A love that seeks only personal benefits is not Divine love.

Sacrificial love has many, many expressions in parenting. To be a parent is to be "a giver." Another way parents give and express love to their children is by the words they speak. The great Christian writer, Andrew Murray, said,

"Let father and mother lead a life marked by love to God and man; this is the atmosphere in which loving children can be trained. Let all the dealings with children be in holy love. Cross words, sharp reproof, impatient answers, are infectious. Love demands, and fears not. Self-sacrifice, time, thoughtful attention, and patient perseverance are needed to train our children aright. Let our children hear us speak of others, friends or enemies, always in a way that will show the love of Christ."

Children learn from their parents so much about what is

good, what is bad, what is helpful, what is degrading. The words used with children should be uplifting. A parent's vocabulary ought to inspire a child, to encourage a child, to elevate a child. A child called "good-for-nothing" will probably conform to that name. Cruel and teasing words spoken by parents to children are one of the main ways of provoking them to wrath or breaking their spirits.

Words carry a powerful force that can determine both the attitudes of children and the atmosphere of a home. Negative, complaining, critical or judgmental words spread emotions and attitudes to other family members. Scripture admonishes,

"Let no corrupt communication proceed out of your mouth, but that which is good to the use of edifying, that it may minister grace unto the hearers" (Ephesians 4:29).

One time of the day to especially guard our speech is at mealtime. The conversation around the table should be positive, wholesome, and edifying. Sharing the faults of others does not help the digestion or the spirit of anyone.

Sacrificial love expresses itself also in time and attention. Many parents never hear what their children say because they do not take the time to listen. The same parents later wonder why their children don't listen to them. To listen to a child does take time; and taking time requires a sacrifice. One thing, one concern, one matter must be given up in order to stop and listen.

Attention, too, is an expression of love. A child needs the close body contact of a parent. The warm, affectionate hug by father or mother can mean more to a child than hundreds of toys or gifts. Parents should not hesitate to show this love, as it is from infancy a child experiences security, a strength and a stability through a father and mother's embrace.

It Is a Love that Is Not Judgmental

God made each of us. And each of us is unique. God does not judge by comparing our abilities or capacities with someone else. God accepts us and loves us for who we are.

God's way of loving us should be remembered when parenting children. To compare a child with another and to say, "Why can't you do as well as so-and-so?" is to judge, to indirectly condemn, and to destroy a child's sense of self-worth. Parents, it can be said, are the ones who instill in their children the personal symbols of success or failure. This is a great responsibility. A parent has the power to make a child experience a feeling of failure or of never being able to accomplish anything worthwhile. To avoid error in this matter it is important for parents to help a child find and fulfill that special talent or unique ability that God has given him.

God measures a person's success in terms of whether or not a person does what God asks him to do. "Well done, thou good and faithful servant: . . . enter thou into the joy of thy lord" (Matthew 25:21). If we limit the definition of success to mean simply the attainment of status or certain income brackets, we fail to understand what God wants done in our lives. God can bless us with these things, but they are not the proof of true success. The success of Jesus was in His obedience to the mission of the Father—and that meant public abuse and ignominious death by crucifixion in order to make atonement for sin. He said His joy came from doing the will of Him who had sent Him. According to contemporary standards of success, Jesus was a failure. He had no money. He had no political status or rank in the community. He earned no medals or trophies. He was, in fact, despised, rejected by men, and even deserted by His friends. But, the Bible tells us God has exalted His Son, having raised Him from the dead and given Him all authority in heaven and on earth.

Most of the early Christians cared little about contemporary standards of success. Stephen, the first martyr of the church, certainly would not pass the success tests of today: he did a poor job of making friends or getting people to like him. He declared to people what God wanted him to say instead of what they wanted to hear. Was he successful? At his death the Bible tells us Jesus stood up to welcome His servant home. Or think of John the Baptist: because he worked out his divine calling he was beheaded. Was he successful? Yet Jesus said of all the prophets there was not one greater than John the Baptist.

Loving parents will encourage children to seek the high standard of God's Word and will for themselves whatever the cost. Children can be taught that in doing God's will there is full and complete joy and contentment. "Whoever will lose his life for my sake," Jesus said, "will surely find it" (see Matthew 10:39).

9

DISCIPLINE
(Part 1)

Love

| Example | "He that spareth his rod hateth his son: but he that loveth him chasteneth him betimes."

Proverbs 13:24 | DISCIPLINE |

Teaching

Why Discipline?

Discipline is an outflow of love. Love is wanting the best for someone. Discipline is a part of loving. "Because I want the best for you I am not going to allow you to do or to be anything that will rob you of that best," a loving parent will say.

Often a parent will remark, "Oh, I love my children too much to discipline them." However, the Bible tells us (see

Proverbs 13:24) *to not* discipline children is to hate them.
This can happen when parents choose to withhold the brief
moment of pain needed for correction and allow children to
continue on in attitudes and actions that will affect their
well-being throughout life. To refuse to discipline children is
a clear sign that we do not have the love God wants us to
have for our children. We are wrong to confuse love with
mere emotion or sentiment. Love, as the Bible speaks of it, is
a conscious commitment to the well-being and betterment of
another. One day when our nine-year-old niece was visiting
our home, she told my wife very cheerfully, "My mommy
spanks me because she loves me."

We need to discipline our children for two very
important reasons. The first one is because they need it.
Proverbs 22:15 says, "Foolishness is bound in the heart of a
child; but the rod of correction shall drive it far from him."
No child is born perfect. Discipline is part of God's way of
bringing a life as early as possible to Him and conforming
that life to His image. "Withhold not correction from the
child: for if thou beatest him with the rod, he shall not die.
Thou shalt beat him with the rod, and shalt deliver his soul
from hell" (Proverbs 23:13,14).

A popular theory today is that a child is born basically
good and innocent, and if a child is left to develop freely, he
will grow up happy and fulfilled. This view teaches that
human society corrupts people; society imposes rules and
requirements that create both guilt and frustration. The
blame for problem children and degenerate adults is to be put
upon the social environment, says this theory. However, the
Bible tells us the real problem is in the human heart.

Many parents accept this theory and believe that the
way to have happy children is to allow them to grow up
without any restraints. They think that happiness can be
found by children through free expression of themselves in
any way that they might choose. They see discipline in any

form as cruelty and parental authority dictatorial. They often prefer to see themselves just as "friends" of their children instead of parents.

The second reason for disciplining children—and the most important reason of all—is because God tells parents to discipline children. And God, as our heavenly Father, likewise disciplines His spiritual children. Hebrews 12:6 says, "For whom the Lord loveth he chasteneth, and scourgeth every son whom he receiveth." Both parents and children must understand that God orders the mother and the father to discipline children. To know that discipline follows from God's command creates in the children not resentment but respect and admiration for parents. As the children grow older, they recognize that discipline came their way as an act of obedience to God, from parents who truly loved them.

Often the major problem in a home is not the children, but the parents. They are the ones who first need disciplining. Often they will put their own human emotions and reasoning ahead of God's instruction. Parents who indiscriminately indulge their children, who regularly give the children what they want whenever they whine or flatter, may think that they are expressing love. But they are not. Actually such parents are cruel: they encourage the children toward selfishness and self-centeredness.

Recently I heard a young lady at a checkout stand chatting with the clerk. "I see you're getting married," said the clerk. "That's right, and I can't wait." "How long do you think it'll be before you have kids?" "Kids! Not me. I won't have those spoiled brats. I can't stand them. No, no kids for me." That woman was not giving a description of children, but a description of what she was, and the kind of parent she would be. Children will become what parents allow them to become.

Discipline is also an act of faith as well as an act of obedience. One mother said she thought faith meant that if you believed hard enough for something it would come to pass. Then she began to realize that faith meant first believing God's Word; second, acting on that Word; and third, knowing that God will do His part by fulfilling His promises to those who believe and obey. This woman said she became certain that, as she was obedient in the daily training and discipline with her children, the Lord would by His Spirit work in their hearts so that they would commit themselves to God's purposes throughout their lives. For her, disciplining in faith meant sticking to the task even though her emotions and her personal inclinations tended toward being indulgent toward her children. She came to see that love, obedience and faith all relate to one another in an active relationship to God and to her children.

"We know that all things work together for good to them that love God, to them who are the called according to his purpose. For whom he did foreknow, he also did predestinate to be conformed to the image of his Son, that he might be the firstborn among many brethren" (Romans 8:28,29).

Once we are settled on the fact that our children need discipline and that God commands it, then we need to know for what purpose we are to discipline. Discipline must be neither sporadic nor haphazard. Discipline is simply a means to an end. The end or goal, however, must be clear. To aim at a bull's-eye helps a target shooter know if his aim is true. An airplane pilot must have his destination clearly in mind in order to set his instruments so that they will help him understand his flight charts. The ultimate goal for a Christian parent is for the children to first personally know and be committed to the Lord Jesus Christ; and second, be testimonies to Christ's life and character.

There are two main areas in a child's life that can threaten the arrival at this goal. The first is the development of *bad attitudes*. The second is *willful disobedience*. Whenever children manifest a bad attitude or are willfully disobedient, they need to be disciplined. And as children learn to obey their parents with a proper attitude, they also learn what it is to obey God. In another sense, discipline forms a mold into which God can pour His Spirit. A child can be formed into a vessel that will be fit for the Master's use.

In his book *You and Your Child*, Charles R. Swindoll says,

> "We deal as severely with attitudes in our home as we do with actions. A sullen, stubborn spirit is dealt with as directly as an act of lying or stealing. The way you deal with your sons will, in great measure, determine how they will respond to the way God deals with them."

God has given man certain boundaries within which to function. The boundary lines are set up by His moral law. God's will for man is not just to live within the boundaries but to live within them *happily*. This happens when man sees that God has not set up these boundaries to be mean or strict or rob man of fun, but rather to keep man from doing those things that dishonor God and bring man into bondage. God's will is a wonderful thing. He has given us rich things to enjoy. He doesn't want people serving Him with a chip on their shoulder or with a feeling of resentment because they think they're missing out in life. Psalm 100:2 tells us, "Serve the Lord with gladness." In the same way it is not enough that children stay within the boundaries their parents' give them, but that they live within them happily. This happiness comes from knowing they are pleasing their parents, and from the assurance of their parents' love that desires only the best for them.

> "Let us hear the conclusion of the whole matter: Fear God, and keep his commandments: for this is the whole duty of man" (Ecclesiastes 12:13).

"He hath shewed thee, O man, what is good;
and what doth the Lord require of thee, but to do
justly, and to love mercy, and to walk humbly with
thy God" (Micah 6:8).

"Children, obey your parents in all things: for this
is well-pleasing unto the Lord" (Colossians 3:20).

Obedience and a right attitude are God's will for every
child. God desires both an outward and an inward conformity to His will. A child's personality or aptitude or sex or
temperament is no excuse for willful disobedience or for an
incorrect attitude. It does not matter whether a child is quiet,
outgoing, athletic, or studious. He still can be trained to be a
happy and obedient child.

What Is Obedience?

Obedience from a child ought to occur whenever a child
is asked to do something by his parents, but in a reasonable
tone of voice—not by screaming or yelling. A friend had her
four-year-old neighbor girl over to her house one day and
after the girl had been there awhile she asked, "Do you
always talk soft?" The little girl's reply: "My mommy
screams."

A child must be taught to respond to his parents'
instruction. A child's own view of what he would rather do,
or whether the parents' words appear reasonable, is
irrelevant. But a child must be taught obedience to the words
of a parent.

Disobedience is a serious issue and should never be
ignored or treated lightly by a parent. First Samuel 15:22,23
says, "And Samuel said, Hath the Lord as great delight in
burnt offerings and sacrifices, as in obeying the voice of the
Lord? Behold, to obey is better than sacrifice, and to hearken
than the fat of rams. For rebellion is as the sin of witchcraft,
and stubbornness is as iniquity and idolatry. Because thou

hast rejected the word of the Lord, he hath also rejected thee from being king."

Parents can shudder at the thought of witchcraft and yet think lightly of disobedience. Some parents have even made the mistake of calling disobedience "cute." I've witnessed parents ask their child to do something and the child refuses, acting shy, batting his eyelashes, and running away. Instead of disciplining the child for not obeying, the parent laughs, "Oh, isn't he cute?" which is supposed to make everything okay. The Bible says, "My son, hear the instruction of thy father, and forsake not the law of thy mother: for they shall be an ornament of grace unto thy head, and chains about thy neck" (Proverbs 1:8,9). (Here let me insert the writer assumes parents are giving their children the proper instruction based upon God's Word, and not instructing them to do evil!)

Actual obedience involves three things or it surely is not obedience. The first is *immediacy*. If you ask your child to do something, like picking up toys, and he says, "Later," or "In a few minutes," and an hour later the toys are still lying about, obedience has not occurred. If the child is asked to pick up the toys *now*, then a parent must expect the child to respond immediately. Quick obedience to a parent's word is vital; and love demands it. A mother who discovers her child playing in the street and sees a car suddenly appear, will call out to her child, "Come here!" She wants him to obey *immediately*. She knows response to her words could save his life, just as the disciples' response to Jesus' command, "Follow me," was immediate and lifesaving: "They straightway left their nets and followed him" (Matthew 4:19,20).

The second thing true obedience requires is *completeness*. If a child is asked to pick up the toys and to make his bed, but only picks up the toys, there has not really been obedience. A complete job requires complete obedience.

"Obey, your parents in all things," Colossians 3:20 puts it, "for this is well-pleasing to the Lord."

The third thing true obedience requires is *willingness*. If a child is asked to pick up the toys and to make his bed, then goes off to do both, but has a long face or whines and complains, again there has not been true obedience. A parent must guard against accepting unwilling compliance as obedience. Psalm 100:2 says, "Serve the Lord with gladness."

Complete, immediate, and *willing* obedience is not a child's mere duty or obligation; it is a child's privilege. It is through obedience to parents, God allows children to show the love they have for Him.

One time a father asked his son to sit down while they were driving in the family car. The boy insisted on standing up in the back seat and blocking the father's view through the rearview mirror. Again, the father firmly asked his son to sit down. Finally the son sat down. A few minutes passed, and suddenly the boy spoke out, "Dad, I'm sitting down on the outside, but I'm standing up on the inside."

Complete obedience means sitting down on the inside as well as the outside!

What Is a Right Attitude?

The proper response to conditions and things around us constitutes what I mean by the right attitude. The proper response is one which is characterized by a happy disposition. Unkind words and unkind acts emerge from a wrong attitude. We can discern bad attitudes as they differ among children at different ages and in different personalities. Parents need to understand a child's attitudes and deal with them for what they are.

When a parent calls the child from another room or from outside, the child should be taught to answer by saying "coming." This response shows immediate obedience, even though it may take him a minute or two to arrive. Also, when parents ask children to do something or not do something, it is right to teach them always to reply. This way they show respect for the parents and others, and in their courtesy to reply show more clearly their attitude of obedience.

Some of the different ways children can show wrong attitudes when asked to do something are:

1. Crying
2. Yelling, "I don't want to"
3. Stomping and kicking of the feet (tantrums)
4. Slamming a door in anger
5. Resisting by stiffening of the body and legs (in smaller children, when put to bed or put in a chair)
6. Pouting
7. Pushing a parent away (for whatever reason)
8. Fussing or whining.

It might help to look at a typical example. A child is told, "It is time for bed now, Tommy."

Tommy goes to his bedroom; but he cries, fusses and rebels. Inwardly he is rebelling and not obedient.

A parent needs to discipline a child in this situation. Even though his feet take him to his room, Tommy needs to learn that obedience requires the attitude of *willing* cooperation. Tommy needs to realize that when he is told to go to bed, there is no other "happy" alternative. Yes, Tommy can accept that, and he will accept it happily, if he knows that his parents love him and will not budge on this matter of going to bed. A child can *choose* to be happy. As a child makes that choice the heart is prepared to receive the joy and peace of God's Spirit.

Once my daughter resisted all efforts to teach her how to sit quietly in church. She would sit on my wife's lap, but push away at my wife's hands and arms as they held her. It became clear that she was inwardly resisting, though outwardly conforming. She was saying by her gestures, "I will sit, but I will sit my own way!"

My wife did not accept that message from our daughter. And by an act of further discipline she made it clear to our daughter that her attitude was wrong and unacceptable. After discipline, our daughter lovingly relaxed in my wife's lap and enjoyed the hour without struggle or resistance. When this area is properly dealt with a parent can fully enjoy the cooperation of the child, whether it's in church, at home, at the store, or at someone else's home.

When Not to Discipline

If a parent does not clearly understand the issues for which discipline is needed, those issues being willful disobedience and wrong attitudes, children might be wrongly or unjustly disciplined. Unjust discipline should be carefully avoided, because it can so badly discourage and frustrate a child. Here are some things for which children should not be disciplined:

Being Themselves—Although obedience and right attitudes are God's universal standard for every life, each person differs from another. Each life is unique. No one that God has made is inferior to anyone else. Each life has its own special personality, abilities, and aptitudes. And God has a special way of revealing Himself through every person. A child must be allowed to discover that special expression of God's love and power within him.

Parents often make the mistake of comparing their children with other children. If one of their children does not measure up to some ability or characteristic possessed by another child, they try to force conformity through discipline.

I have discovered times when my own pride, rather than my children's willful disobedience, has caused me to react wrongly to them. Sometimes, because of selfish pride, a parent will put undue pressure upon a child so that the parent can boast to others of his child's accomplishments. A parent must learn to walk the fine line between encouraging excellence in performance and demanding a perfection that a child simply cannot achieve.

Another related way in which a child can be wrongly disciplined is to rush a child into an area of growth or maturity for which he is not ready. Sometimes children can be asked to do things they don't have the physical or mental ability to do. If so, this is not willful disobedience, and it should never be seen as an occasion for discipline. The Bible says, "Foolishness is bound in the heart of a child; but the rod of correction shall drive it far from him" (Proverbs 22:15). But childishness is not foolishness. Foolishness is an inward attitude of carelessness, indifference and disrespect for the ways of God. Childishness is simply being like a child. It is being unreflective, spontaneous, enthusiastic, and naive. There is nothing wrong with that. Paul says, "When I was a child I spake as a child, I understood as a child, I thought as a child: but when I became a man, I put away childish things" (1 Corinthians 13:11). Childishness is only wrong when it is practiced by an adult. But a child should never be forced to act like an adult. Nor should a parent expect a two-year-old to act like a five-year-old, or a five-year-old to act like a ten-year-old. There is nothing wrong with being a child. Parents are to enjoy their children for what they are at every age.

When You Are Angry or Impatient—It is possible for a child to upset or frustrate a parent by simply being a child, and that is when a parent needs patience, not the means for discipline. A baby cries because he is sick, hungry, or wet. A child in all innocence might do something wrong that he intended to do right. One time a girl put her father's wet shoes in the oven to dry. The shoes dried, but they could not be worn again. Yet the girl's intention was to please and to help her father.

Sometimes a child by accident will drop a glass of water or bump into a shelf of knickknacks and knock them to the floor. Mistakes, misjudgments, accidents are all a part of growing and learning. And even parents have accidents, remember. A parent must never make a child feel guilty over something about which the child did not have normal control or about which the limitations of childhood caused the mistake or misjudgment.

A child bursting into the house full of excitement and bubbling over to tell about a new discovery or about a bruised and skinned knee, may not notice mother is talking to someone on the telephone. To react in anger to such an interruption and to discipline the child for his exuberance and spontaneity is wrong. It would be better for the mother, if possible, to excuse herself from her conversation on the telephone and take a moment to acknowledge and enjoy this loud and exuberant gift from God. After all, the interruption is but for a moment, unintentional, and a sign that the child runs to one he loves with either joy or pain.

Legitimate Forgetfulness—There are times when children innocently forget to do something that has been asked of them. For example, in a child's excitement to go to the park with the family for a picnic, he may innocently forget to bring the jug of cold drink a parent asked him to fetch from the refrigerator. This is not willful disobedience and a parent's response in these times should manifest understanding rather than irritation.

When Uncertain of the Issue—A child should not be disciplined if a parent is not sure, exactly, what took place during a specific incident. A parent should not react hastily, but be careful to get all the facts first. A child comes into the house crying, claiming a brother or sister hit him. Without all the facts this incident could appear that the child was deliberately struck as a result of a brother or sister's anger or meanness. However, after further questioning, the parent discovers that facts revealed the child was hit by a ball the brother or sister was playing with, and that it accidentally hit the child when it bounced. Without correct facts a child could be disciplined unfairly.

10

DISCIPLINE
(Part 2)

Love

┌─────────────────────────┐
│   │
│ "My son, forget not my │
│ law; but let thine heart│
│ keep my commandment." │
│   Proverbs 3:1 │
│   │
└─────────────────────────┘

Example   DISCIPLINE

Teaching

Establishing Obedience in a Child

It is surprising how closely happiness in a child is connected to obedience. A happy child is an obedient child. God has called children to be obedient, and as they come into harmony with God's will for them, happiness is the outcome.

To train a child to be obedient, it is best and easiest to start as early as possible; and conversely, the best time to begin to discipline a child is when you discern he is willfully disobeying or manifesting a rebellious attitude. Normally, once a child begins to start crawling or walking, his comprehension is developed enough to deal with what a parent knows to be unacceptable behavior.

In order to get an early and effective start with children, parents need to get together and agree on certain house rules concerning acceptable and unacceptable behavior. Knowing the goals, which are 1) knowing and serving Christ and 2) development of Christlike character, helps to determine the house rules. And these also provide guidelines for acceptable behavior.

House rules are like a pole that is placed along side a young plant growing in the garden. The pole is not there to stop the plant's development, but to help guide it into maturity and productivity.

House rules provide an important base from which to develop obedience. It lets a child know where he stands and helps to create both a sense of freedom and security. A child does not really care which house rules are made, but he does need to know *what* they are. There is no right or wrong set of house rules. The rules are a matter of husband and wife determining together what they want for their household. It is better to establish a small list of rules and stick by those rather than to make a long list of rules and only live consistently by a few of them.

One house rule my wife and I decided on before our first child was born was that our household arrangement of furniture would always remain the same. We would not rearrange our furniture to accommodate a child. Books, furniture, knickknacks would remain where they were.

When our son came to a crawling age, we let him know that we were not going to rearrange the house simply because he had entered our lives. He was going to have to learn to fit into our plans instead of us fitting into his. We communicated this to him and it helped him get off to a right start by establishing him with a set of limits and arrangements of his household world. He also learned quickly what was acceptable and unacceptable behavior.

The way to communicate your house rules to your child at a young age is by saying "no" to your child when he is about to break a rule. Posting the rules does no good at all. Nor does a long explanation or justification for a rule help. The word "no" is the most effective and the simplest way of letting him know what is not acceptable either in his conduct or disposition. The word "no" can be established before the toddler stage and will be reinforced with discipline when he begins to move about. Before our first child reached one year he was actively moving about the house. One day he headed for the coffee table where we kept some magazines he was not allowed to take. As he reached for the magazines, I said, "No." He stopped a moment, looked at me, then turned around and grabbed the magazines. It was clear he understood my disapproval, yet when I repeated "no," he still went after the magazines. Through discipline he was quickly introduced to the meaning of the word "no" when it applied to the magazines.

When I took my son back to the living room, he went straight for the magazines a second time. I said "no" again. He hesitated, then lunged toward the magazines. Again, I firmly corrected him and returned him to the living room. On his third trip toward the magazines, I spoke firmly, saying, "No." This time he hesitated, looked at me, looked at the magazines, and headed off in another direction.

Even at this young age he was testing me. He wanted to know his limits. But the early agreement between my wife and me helped our son to find his place and his limits within the family. This experience also helped to establish the authority of our word and to let him know when we said the word "no" we meant it. But it also taught him the areas of free movement within the home. He came to know that to cross a certain line of unacceptable behavior was wrong. But he could freely do many other things without crossing that line.

Another house rule my wife and I established was that at mealtimes the children were to eat what they were served. Of course, we had to be careful to give them reasonable servings and to make sure that they hadn't ruined their appetite by snacking before a meal. It was easier, we learned, to give our children second helpings than to overload their plates and to expect them to finish the food.

Meals may seem to be an insignificant area for discipline. But attention to little things contributes to a child's need to know what it means to complete any given task. Jesus, in a parable, spoke of great honor and reward to those faithful servants of His who do the little things God gives them to do:

> "And it came to pass, that when he was returned, having received the kingdom, then he commanded these servants to be called unto him, to whom he had given the money, that he might know how much every man had gained by trading. Then came the first, saying, Lord, thy pound hath gained ten pounds. And he said unto him, Well, thou good servant: because thou hast been faithful in a very little, have thou authority over ten cities" (Luke 19:15-17).

Strong character traits are developed as attention is given to the little things. We felt the issue of our children finishing the food on their plate was helping to develop thoroughness in their character by teaching them the importance of finishing what they start.

Often mealtime provides an excellent opportunity to learn some valuable lessons for parents as well as children. One time at the dinner table, I received a lesson in law and grace. Our children had known our house rule about finishing their food and they were learning to abide by it. During a particular meal, it became very difficult for one of the children to finish his food. I saw the struggle going on, but I wasn't sure if the reason for the struggle was because he had been overserved or because he was not well, or because he was just stubborn. Everyone at the table knew our rule, yet I didn't know whether discipline was needed. I sat with my dilemma for some time. Finally, I did the only thing I knew to do. I reminded the children that our rule was food on a plate had to be eaten. So to satsify the rule, I took the remaining portion and finished it myself. The house rule was fulfilled, and the child was released.

This incident, although it only repeated itself one other time in our family, revealed to me a fresh insight concerning Christ's sacrifice on the cross. I saw that when He died and took my sins, He was satsifying the demands of God's law. He took my place and bore my sin so that I could be free. The cross was law and grace in action. One of the greatest joys of being a parent is the discovery of God's love, and the opportunities parenthood provides of acting out that love for children.

The dinner table can also be a valuable place to train a child in other important areas of character. One of these areas is thankfulness. A great sin of the people of Israel, the Bible tells us, was to constantly murmur and complain. And most of the time that complaining was about food and water. God strongly disciplined them for their unthankful hearts and warns us not to follow their example. The New Testament says, "Do all things without murmurings and disputings: that ye may be blameless and harmless, the sons of God, without rebuke, in the midst of a crooked and perverse nation, among whom ye shine as lights in the world" (Philippians 2:14,15).

A child does not have to like everything that he is given to eat. But as a member of the family, he should learn to eat what everyone else eats. A mother need not make a separate meal for each child in the family. A child needs to learn to appreciate the tastes and likes of others. Catering to the special tastes and desires of each child for every meal not only creates a fussy and picky attitude toward food, but encourages an expectation of special treatment in other areas of life.

Another occasion for discipline that contributes to Christian character is the church service. Christian worship with other believers provides a perfect environment for reinforcing the lessons a child learns in the home.

When I first began to carry our small children into church, I could count on a panic-stricken usher to race over to our pew to steer us in the direction of a cry-room or nursery.

"No thanks," I'd say. "We prefer to keep our children with us in church."

I wanted our children to fit into and to adapt to our lives and to our Christian commitment. Church was a place we attended weekly; and our children needed to learn to act in an acceptable manner in a church environment. They were not to see church time as another playtime. Church time was to become for them a time of quiet, of reverence, of respectfulness. We found that a child *can* learn to sit still, even for an hour, if the parents determine that sitting still is proper. A child does not need to be free to walk up and down the aisles, to play with hymnbooks, or to have a supply of toys to play with in order to be quiet and happy. Whenever our children began to fuss in church, we reminded them once that such behavior was unacceptable. If they continued, they were taken out, disciplined, and returned to the pew. A simple guideline we found was that if a child must be taken out of church because of disobedience, fussiness, or rowdiness, a parent must make it uncomfortable for the child. To take a fussy child out and then to allow the child to play instead of being disciplined, simply reinforces the fussy behavior. Next time the child will fuss again in church just to get to a better place. The principle is to make it so unpleasant out of church that the child wants to get back into church and sit respectfully.

After establishing conduct rules, it is important that the word "no" spoken in a firm but normal voice be understood. Remember, good rules may be set down, but if children don't listen to your word, trouble remains. The word "no" is how a parent begins to communicate house rules. It is the one word that communicates what is not acceptable behavior. Yet children must obey every word of a parent given as instruction or command; "come here" or "sit still," for example.

In training for obedience there are rules parents will establish which will always stay the same. For example, parents may want a rule in the house that says "no jumping on the furniture." This is a set rule that will remain year after year. But there are times when a child may ask something, such as "Mommy, may I have a cookie?" Sometimes a parent will say "yes" and sometimes "no," but this is where he learns to obey your word.

Once a parent asks a child to do something the child should learn to obey the first time he is asked, and this may only happen if the child knows the parent means what has been said.

One day a mother called to her son who was playing in the yard, with a neighbor boy. "It's time for lunch—come on in and eat, Johnny," she called. Johnny ignored the request and kept playing. Several minutes later the mother called out again, "Johnny, didn't you hear me? I said come and eat." Still Johnny ignored the call. After the third time, Johnny's friend said, "Hey, aren't you going to go in to eat?" "No," said Johnny. "Mom doesn't mean it until she says, 'Johnny Robert Allen, you come in here!' "

If a child asks, "May I go to Johnny's house and play?"

and you say "no," but five or ten minutes later he is back asking the same question, his behavior indicates he has not taken your answer as final and will probably ask you over and over hoping maybe on the fifth time around you'll give in and say "yes." Teach children to accept no as the answer the *first* time they ask. As a way of clarifying the answer a parent could say, "No you won't be playing at Johnny's house today." This makes it clear that there's no need to ask that particular question again today. Another way to clarify an answer could be something like this: "Mommy, can we watch TV?" "Not now, children, I'll let you know when you can watch it, so you don't need to ask me anymore. I'll let you know when it's okay to turn it on." This settles a series of questions every few minutes.

I was in a store one day standing next to a woman in the jewelry department. Her child was sitting upon the counter near a spinner rack of watch bands. The child began to spin the rack while the mother looked at some merchandise. The mother saw her son playing, and said, "Stop that."

The boy continued to spin the rack.

"Stop, I said."

The boy continued.

"No candy for you," the mother said.

The boy continued spinning the rack.

For over five minutes the mother watched her son, threatened him, and tried to concentrate on the merchandise she was examining. She failed to carry out anything she threatened to do to her disobedient child. The boy won the contest. And the mother went away angry and frustrated.

The word "no" needs to communicate firmness and control. Too often children are asked to respond only to an emotional reaction on the part of a parent rather than to a word. Parents, often out of frustration, react in anger toward their children. They discipline their children only when they themselves have reached a point of anger. Only when they are out of control emotionally can they get their children to obey. A curious contradiction which any child soon sees through occurs when his parents expect to control him when they cannot control themselves.

The Bible speaks with great wisdom when it says to let our "yes" be "yes" and our "no" mean "no" (see Matthew 5:37). A lot of parental speaking amounts literally to "vain words"—that is, warnings are given, but no action is taken. There is no meaning behind the words, so no child listens. If a parent has to say "no" ten times before some action is taken, the child is learning to obey on the tenth time around. A parent's "no" should mean "no" the first time. If a child is not disciplined until the parent is angry, the child learns to obey only when a parent gets angry. If a parent gets angry and frustrated and does nothing, the child learns not to obey at all.

Another mistake parents make is trying to reason with their children instead of having them obey their word. When a parent tries to reason with a child, the parent usually ends up losing. A child does not need to be persuaded by reason. The logic of a parent's argument often does nothing but frustrate both parent and child. A child wants to have his own way. He is not concerned about doing what is reasonable.

A parent once wanted his children to play in a part of the house other than the living room. Play in the living room disturbed the adult conversation. Instead of simply asking the children to go play in another part of the house, this parent entered into a reasoning session.

"Wouldn't it be nice if you played somewhere else?" he said.

"We like it here," replied the children.

"But think how much fun it would be to play in the den where some of your bigger toys are," insisted the parent.

"But we are having fun here," said the children.

The dialogue continued for several minutes. Finally, in frustration, the parent turned to the only thing he knew could get the result he wanted—the bribe! "Okay, kids, you go play in the den, and I'll fix you each a big ice cream cone."

Such reasoning sessions often end with a bribe of this sort. The bribe is not only shameful behavior for an adult, but it ruins a child's character. If a child learns to do the thing a parent asks only for what he can get out of it, the child soon takes a "what's in it for me?" attitude toward other more serious matters.

Jesus said that the greatest among people were to be those who had become the servants to all. A servant is not motivated by self-interest. A servant is motivated by a maximum concern for others. The highest motive a child can have is the desire to please and to honor his parents. Training for obedience is linked to service to God later in life. As a child develops a heart for service, happiness comes from seeing others helped. True happiness continues in life as the child begins to seek to please the Lord by serving those God brings into his life.

Nipping Things in the Bud

A good piece of advice from an old gardener friend of mine is to nip things in the bud. It is a simple thing to pull up a little seedling with only a few small roots. But if you wait until you have a big tree, it is a big job to pull the tree out. It can be done. But it requires expensive machinery. So, when you see actions beginning to develop in your child that you know are wrong or dangerous—whether it's a laxness toward your word or something negative in their attitude—it is best to deal with situations immediately. Ignoring a problem will not cause it to go away. Don't let problems grow, hoping they will go away. Don't think that one day when you don't have a headache, or when your schedule is lighter, that you can deal with it. The longer a problem area remains, the larger it grows and the more costly and time-consuming will be its resolution.

The most effective way of nipping problems in the bud is by being consistent. Be consistent in abiding by house rules. Be consistent in expecting obedience when you speak. Be consistent in enforcing rules.

Inconsistency, for whatever reason, creates confusion for children. If "no" means "no" today it should still mean "no" tomorrow for whatever issue it applies to. Children actually depend upon and want consistency from their parents for order in their lives. Sometimes inconsistency stems from a parent's laziness or disobedience to God's Word, when it's just too much trouble to do what is required, and so things slip by. Parents must stand by the rules they make and the things they ask of their children. Every time a violation of the house rules or a willful disobedience takes place, parents must follow through with discipline.

But how does a parent know when obedience has been achieved through his consistent discipline? The answer is, when children do what they are told to with a cooperative attitude.

What Is Discipline?

When it is time to reinforce training with discipline the Bible teaches what form of discipline should be used. Proverbs 29:15 says, "The rod and reproof give wisdom: but a child left to himself bringeth his mother to shame." Proverbs 22:15 says, "Foolishness is bound in the heart of a child; but the rod of correction shall drive it far from him."

God's way of discipline for parents is to spank a child with a rod. This is the most loving, constructive form of discipline that there is. Putting a child in the corner for an hour or taking away his supper or yelling at him or giving him a tongue-lashing or calling him a variety of names, all fall short of God's way of discipline. Discipline of children with a rod, if it issues from love and concern for the child's best, is right and good. This type of discipline comes from a parent who, from a heart of faith, obeys God.

Spanking should be done in love and with control. It should not be done in selfish anger or rage. A spanking given in love is not child abuse. Child abuse results from frustration, and it indicates a parent has simply lost control. Child abuse is a symptom of a deeper problem that a parent has with himself or herself. It is usually the result of unloving parents striking out at their children in anger over some more personal frustration. Because the parent is out of control personally, the children are also out of control and the frustration is compounded. A spanking ought to be an act of love, not of violence, or anger, or rage. A spanking ought to communicate to a child both a parent's displeasure and a parent's concern and love. A spanking is not a form of parental strictness or parental punishment. A spanking is a form of parental love that chooses to deal with the issues that God instructs them to deal with in order to bring about the peaceable fruits of righteousness in their children's lives.

Spanking with a rod in love on a child's bottom (which is the place God has provided for a spanking) creates a healthy and right kind of fear in a child. A child learns to fear doing what is wrong instead of fearing his parents. When parents respond to their children in anger and explode in fits of rage, shout cruel words or physically abuse their children, the child learns to fear his parents more than the wrong he has done. The right kind of fear in a child opens the heart up to receive true instruction in wisdom and helps establish it in the fear of the Lord. "The fear of the Lord is the beginning of wisdom" (Psalm 111:10). "The fear of the Lord is to hate evil" (Proverbs 8:13). A true fear of the Lord doesn't create a desire in the heart to depart from God but to depart from evil. True fear of the Lord is the result of God's love for us and our love for Him. Because we love Him we want to keep ourselves from doing those things which will hurt Him. Because God loves us He desires to keep us from those things which will hurt us.

Andrew Murray in his book, *The Children for Christ*, says,

"A cause of parental weakness is the good-natured weakness, misnamed kindness, which cannot bear ever to reprove, to thwart, or to punish a child. This is nothing but a form of slothfulness, a parental attitude that refuses to assume responsibility to God or child. Parents do not realize that indirectly they choose the greater pain of seeing children grow up unrestrained. No grace of the Christian life is obtained without sacrifice; this very high grace of influencing and forming other souls for God needs special self-sacrifice. Like every difficult work, it needs purpose, attention and perseverance."

The reason spanking with a rod is the most loving way to discipline is that it is the most effective way of dealing with the problem of disobedience and wrong attitudes. God in His loving wisdom commands parents to spank their children with a rod. It is the quickest and surest way to obedience and happiness in our children.

Punishment, unlike discipline with a rod, deprives a child of some privilege or reward (such as an allowance or a trip or a snack) but does not really deal with the issues of the heart; and often creates bitterness and resentment in the child. There is nothing wrong with a child receiving rewards for achievement, but should not become the means whereby parents deal with willful disobedience and wrong attitudes in their children.

Strictness, unlike discipline with a rod, creates harshness and rigidity in the home resulting in bondage and condemnation for a child that destroys his inward joy.

Yelling and name-calling are not loving discipline because they only crush a child's spirit and don't motivate a child toward improvement, or to accomplish the exciting things God has for him. Attacking a child's identity by disparaging him or humiliating him causes him to lose self-worth. To say, "You good for nothing," or "You brat," or "You're impossible," creates feelings of inferiority and a sense of uselessness and discouragement.

Rather, it is important to deal directly with the naughtiness by saying, "That is disobedience" or "This attitude is self-pity" or "You lied, and lying is a sin." There is a real difference between dealing with the sin issue and with attacking a personality. Some people go through their adult life with great feelings of resentment or a sense of guilt and condemnation, because they were never lovingly disciplined with a rod when they were a child.

A rod is a flexible twig or branch from a tree. It is the most effective instrument for giving a spanking because it produces the greatest amount of pain with the least amount of injury. To inflict pain on a child's bottom is not cruelty; pain itself can serve a purpose. If a spanking did not hurt, there would be no reason to administer it. It is meant to be painful (though it ought not to be physically damaging) in order to discourage misbehavior.

"For whom the Lord loveth he chasteneth, and scourgeth every son whom he receiveth. . . . Now no chastening for the present seemeth to be joyous, but grievous: nevertheless afterward it yieldeth the peaceable fruit of righteousness unto them which are exercised thereby. . . . Looking diligently lest any man fail of the grace of God; lest any root of bitterness springing up trouble you, and thereby many be defiled" (Hebrews 12:6,11,15).

A swat with the hand is not a spanking, nor are two or three swats. Proverbs 23:13,14 says, "Withhold not correction from the child: for if thou beatest him with the rod, he shall not die. Thou shalt beat him with the rod, and shalt deliver his soul from hell." In his book, *The Christian Family*, Larry Christenson says that a spanking is an *event*. And so it should be. When a child willfully disobeys, or manifests a wrong attitude, that is the time to spank. And spank him with the "rod." Boards, spoons, belts, etc., can do more physical damage and inflict less pain, even though they may make a loud noise when used. Someone recently shared they had been using Ping Pong paddles and flimsy belts for spanking and didn't really get the desired results of obedience from their children; now that they've started using a stick from a tree they're seeing results coming quickly and a change in attitude almost overnight. Spanking with the hand is not good either. A rod is an impersonal object, and it will not do serious damage to either parent or child.

A mother recently shared with me the struggle she had over whether she should spank her children when they had misbehaved or try to reason with them. One day she was at the sink doing dishes when she felt God speaking to her. The thought came to her that if God had already told her in His Word to spank her children, why was she struggling so? In that moment she said the matter of spanking was permanently settled. Today her children are happy and obedient. And her family harmony testifies to the soundness of her decision to obey God.

Spanking should be done by both parents. A mother needs to spank her children when she is with them; she should not have to wait until her husband arrives at home. Children are to obey both parents. Let me repeat Colossians 3:20: "Children, obey your *parents* in all things: for this is well-pleasing unto the Lord." A spanking needs to be given immediately after a child has been willfully disobedient or manifested a wrong attitude. If discipline occurs many hours later, young children will not remember what they are being spanked for. Moreover, it is cruel to allow the child to worry for hours, waiting for the time when he will be disciplined. And finally, prompt punishment quickly discourages children from repeating acts of disobedience. Ecclesiastes 8:11 warns, "Because sentence against an evil work is not executed speedily, therefore the heart of the sons of men is fully set in them to do evil."

It is best for parents not to spank their children in front of others. It should be a private matter between parent and child. It could cause a child embarrassment that could lead to resentment. Keep it a private affair. Take the child to a room separated from others and close the door. If a child misbehaves in a public place, take him to your car, or go to the nearest private room, for the needed discipline of the spanking.

A helpful suggestion of getting the best results when giving a spanking is to have the child in a good posture to receive the spanking. This can be done in one of two ways. When the child is small he can be bent over the parent's knee. When the child gets bigger it is best for the child to bend over a bed or a chair so that the parent is free to administer the spanking more effectively. Usually when a bigger child is over the parent's knee the parent isn't mobile enough to administer a hard enough spanking to bring repentance.

It is important that when a child is spanked direct contact is made with the child's bottom. Spanking through diapers or heavy jeans does not bring the desired results. Instead the child is only angered and frustrated. Parents must understand the purpose of spanking. It is to bring pain in order to produce repentence. That is God's way of dealing with the heart issue within the child. "Foolishness is bound in the heart of a child; but the rod of correction shall drive it far from him" (Proverbs 22:15). To bring a child to a place of repentance is important. And repentance (*metanoia* in Greek) means turning, doing an about-face, going in the opposite direction. A child needs to be "turned around" in his behavior and his attitude when disobedience has occurred.

A spanking brings attention to the wrong that was done, but it does not condemn the child. It is, in fact, a great way to build a child's sense of self-worth because it demonstrates a parental desire and love to keep the child from evil. Denying a child a privilege or sending him to a room allows the disobedient attitude to remain in the heart and to fester. Punishment such as confinement brings remorse but not repentance. A child will be sorry because of being caught, but not sorry for what was done. Repentance, remember, means to turn around, to change direction 180 degrees.

Spanking must be done long enough and hard enough to bring repentance. "Chasten thy son while there is hope, and let not thy soul spare for his crying" (Proverbs 19:18). A spanking should not stop until a parent senses by the child's cry that repentance has occurred. The first swats usually bring cries of anger or outrage. The child says, in effect, "How dare you spank me!" If you stop at that point, you have accomplished nothing. You must go beyond those first swats and continue until the cry turns to a cry of "I am sorry for what I did." A parent can discern when the rebellious attitude has left the child. Another way of knowing there is true repentance is the willingness of the child after a spanking to go back and make right anything that he has done wrong; that is, if it is possible to do so. This is called restitution, and Matthew 3:8 says, "Bring forth therefore fruits meet for repentance." If a child was unkind to a brother or sister, there should be the confession, "I am sorry." If there was disobedience, the child should then go back and do what he was asked to do. If a child refuses to apologize or to do the thing asked in the first place, or if the child continues to have a grudging attitude, then the child has not been brought to a place of repentance.

Once my wife was spanking our son over an issue of disobedience. In her haste to get the spanking over with she had him bend over and spanked him with his jeans on. He let out an appropriate number of cries, but afterward turned to my wife and said, "Mommy, you better spank me again and let me pull down my jeans. It didn't hurt enough."

Our son confirmed to us through that experience that he needed to be spanked so it hurt in order to bring him the inner release that repentance brings. The Bible warns fathers not to provoke their children to wrath (see Ephesians 6:4). One of the sure ways of provoking a child to wrath is by not thoroughly spanking to the point of bringing repentance. A few swats usually make a child angry and leaves him frustrated.

In *The Christian Family*, Larry Christenson says, "Many parents make the mistake of failing to carry through with a really hard spanking. We think of the scriptural admonition, 'Do not provoke your children to anger,' and we hold back. But what is it that provokes a child to anger? It is discipline which merely irritates, a nagging, indecisive, half-hearted discipline. If you spank your child only enough to make him angry and rebellious, you have not carried out thorough, scriptural discipline. The spanking must go beyond the point of anger. It must evoke a wholesome fear in the child. When an honest fear of his father's authority and discipline occupies a child's mind, he will have no room left for anger. This, again, is nothing but an accurate reflection of the way in which God Himself deals with us, His children. 'It is a fearful thing to fall into the hands of the living God' [Hebrews 10:31]."

"Little David was getting under his mother's feet while she was ironing. 'Go away,' she said, 'Mama is busy.' A few minutes later he was back under her foot. This time she implemented her words with a swat across the bottom. David scampered off, but a few minutes later he was back under her feet, whining and complaining. 'David, Mama is busy! Now go away!' Two swats. Three minutes later, repeat performance. On it went. Grandpa was sitting by, watching all this. Finally he spoke up and said, 'Sandra, a spanking is an event. You're simply abusing that child!' Sandra got the idea. The next time David came back, she took him by the hand, led him into the bedroom, where they had an 'event.' That was the end of it. No more whining and complaining; no more nagging, scolding and swatting. One spanking, soundly administered, will render unnecessary hours of nagging, shouting, arguing, and threatening.

"Parents will never have a clear-cut approach to the discipline of their children until they accept the rod as God's appointed means of discipline. It is the choice of His wisdom and His fatherly love. When a parent finds himself shirking the responsibility which God gives him at this point, shrinking from it because of his own feelings or reasoning, let him set God's Word above his own feelings and reason: 'Do not withhold discipline from a child, if you beat him with a rod, he will not die. If you beat him with a rod you will save his life from hell' [Proverbs 23:13,14].

"Consider. One day we must stand before the judgment seat of Christ [2 Corinthians 5:10] and answer for the way in which we have raised our children. 'What did you do with the children I entrusted to your care? Did you raise them according to my Word?' God has ordained issues of the greatest importance to hinge upon the discipline of the rod—even involving the child's eternal salvation.

"Being a parent is an awesome responsibility. That is why God has provided clear instructions to help us accomplish His purposes. Only the unwise would leave the safety of this 'ark' which God has provided, and follow instead the prescription of a sick and dying world. Yet that is precisely what two generations of parents have done. They have left the clear and time-tested wisdom of the Bible, and entrusted the destiny of their children to a slapdash of contrived opinion. The veneer of intellectual sophistication in the so-called 'modern approach to child-raising' (it was going on in Bible times, too, and was dismissed as the way of the fool) has ensnared many a parent, but it hasn't fooled the children one bit. They caught onto it right away, and have run circles around their befuddled parents."

Another wonderful thing we see about the benefits of spanking is that it ends the hostility in a child. A book with which I am familiar provides a classic example of how *not* to end hostility. For his disobedience a mother sent her boy to his room. While there the boy generated within himself resentment and hatred toward his mother for sending him there. He got out a pencil and paper and began to draw hateful pictures of his mother showing different ways he could get back at her. Yet when the mother discovered what her child had done, she only made a joke of it.

A spanking ends hostility in a child because it deals with the heart issue immediately and does not extend the discipline over a long period of time. When the spanking is over with, the issue ends. A child can walk away with a sense of freedom and release.

Our son has the responsibility of the animals (1 dog, 2 cats). It's his responsibility (when he's home) to train the dog. One day the dog dug a hole under the fence and we had been training the dog not to do this. This particular time Joey was home so it was his responsibility to correct the dog, which he did ever so firmly and lovingly. Soon after the correction, my wife went into the yard and started to scold the dog for what it had done. Just then our boy said, "Mom, I've already corrected her. It's over so don't scold her now. You don't do that to us." My wife realized our son had come to understand that once a matter has been dealt with correctly it should be forgotten and considered in the past.

If spankings have been needed repeatedly there may be marks on the child's bottom from the rod. When our first child was young and needed a few spankings one day, my wife felt embarrassed to have anyone find out. She was afraid someone would think her cruel. We were at a friend's home later that day and her friend did see the marks on his bottom. When my wife admitted her embarrassment, her friend replied by saying, "It's better to have the marks on his bottom now as they will quickly fade away. But the naughtiness if not dealt with will be with him throughout his life." It was just the words my wife needed to hear at that time. Proverbs 20:30 says, "The blueness of a wound cleanseth away evil: so do stripes the inward parts of the belly." And Proverbs 29:17 says, "Correct thy son, and he shall give thee rest; yea, he shall give delight unto thy soul." Our boy has been a real blessing to us and has brought continued joy, as we have seen him so tenderly respond to the Lord and show forth the fruits of the Spirit in our home.

There may be times when a child fights a spanking and will not yield to the rod. This must be dealt with as a separate issue. Suppose a child disobeys and then fights the spanking he deserves. He should be spanked for the initial disobedience and then again for fighting the spanking.

"Correction is grievous unto him that forsaketh the way: and he that hateth reproof shall die. Hell and destruction are before the Lord: how much more then the hearts of the children of men? A scorner loveth not one that reproveth him: neither will he go unto the wise" (Proverbs 15:10-12).

Children may enter a period when they stubbornly fight spankings. They may even hold on to the spanking stick and refuse to let go. Or they may kick and twist themselves around to miss the rod. This, too, is a separate issue. It should be explained to the child that fighting a spanking is rebellion and that the child can learn to receive the spanking willingly. Our daughter went through a period where she resisted a spanking in this way. After disciplining her several times for her resistance, her attitude quickly changed. We've seen God's wisdom work so effectively in her life. As she entered school age, year after year her teachers would especially comment to us what a joy she was to have in class because she was always so happy and content. One teacher said, "She'd be happy anywhere because she's happy inside."

Spanking brings a child freedom from wanting to have his own way and being ruled by his moods and emotions. Children who are spoiled through natural love become disobedient, slothful, greedy, unthankful, and a slave to their own way. The biggest enemy of the spoiled child is himself. He takes his discontent and unhappiness with him wherever he goes. "The rod and reproof give wisdom: but a child left to himself bringeth his mother to shame" (Proverbs 29:15).

If you allow your child to have his own way when you

have told him to do something, or if you allow him to sulk and to complain because he does not want to obey, not only does the child make himself miserable, but he makes the whole household miserable too. A child's uncooperative attitude and behavior, if not corrected, will bring much shame to parents both at home and in public. To allow a child to go his own way brings much grief and heaviness to parents.

We have a friend who was a kindergarten teacher. She has said it was interesting each year to see the kids come into the classroom the first week of school. Within this short amount of time she saw how most of them had learned to get their own way. They each had their own little techniques to achieve this. One would cry and get real sad, another would bat her eyelashes, another would be cranky, another would put up a fuss and protest. Since these techniques had worked so effectively at home, they felt the same techniques would now work with the teacher. Fathers especially should guard against allowing their daughters to have their own way by using their feminine charms. There's nothing wrong with being feminine, but when it's used as a means of getting one's own way, then it is being misused.

A spanking is not over after the rod is put down. It is vital that a time of reconciliation take place before the parent and child leave one another. One time I went to spank my child and after the spanking dropped the rod and went back into the living room saying to myself, "I've done my job." My wife looked at me and said, "You are not finished." I said, "What do you mean?" She said, "Your son needs you." He was still in the bedroom crying. Then I realized something—when God disciplines us He doesn't just leave us, He restores us. There is cleansing and reconciliation. A child needs assurance that the situation that required spanking is now over with, that you forgive him, and that he is not rejected.

After a reasonable amount of crying has occurred after a spanking, a parent should see that the child ends his crying. Much crying leads to self-pity. This too is why a parent should not immediately leave a child alone after a spanking. Often a child will run to the other parent for sympathy and pity and sometimes will get some. This too should be guarded against.

After the crying is a very special time for a parent and child to hug and embrace one another. A child should be reassured of his parent's love. Just as God cleanses and forgives us when we sin once we have repented and confessed that sin, so children should know that their parents forgive them for their offenses. A brief time of prayer together is also meaningful after the spanking.

Consistency

Some people grow discouraged about disciplining their children because they feel it simply does not work. People say, "I'm spanking my kids and I'm not getting results." As an example, a parent tells the child to go to bed. Five minutes later the child is up and walking through the living room. The parent turns around and puts the child back in bed. In a few minutes the child gets up again. By now the parent starts to get upset. The parent's anger starts building up—the cycle is repeated a third time. Now the parent gives a swat and says, "I told you to get to bed, now get in there!" The child begins to fuss and gets cranky. The parent gives the child another quick swat and tells him to be quiet. The child only gets fussier and so the parent in frustration allows the child to stay up a little longer. This type of discipline has only irritated the child and not brought him to the place of obedience.

If spanking does not help to bring about happiness and obedience in children, it is usually because of one of two reasons. The first is that spanking is not done correctly, as in the above illustration. Either it is not done for a long enough time or it is not done hard enough to bring about repentance. The second reason is because of inconsistency. Each parent must be committed to spanking as a form of discipline. Spanking as a form of discipline must be a settled matter in each parent's minds and will. It must not be abandoned when one parent or the other feels emotionally tired. Once house rules are set, parents must stick by them. Once a word has been given to a child, parents must expect that word to be obeyed.

I received the following letter from a young mother which shares how she and her husband came to settle this issue in their hearts. "For about 3 weeks we decided to slack off on our discipline due to paper-thin walls in our apartment. Through that time God showed us His way (the rod) is the only way. In this time there was chaos in our household. Well, this really showed us that faith is obedience to God's Word and we were missing out. We found no matter what the circumstance we must first be obedient to the truth God has already given us in order to grow in faith. We have decided if we do nothing else but train our children, at present, it will be the best way we could use our time. Since we have come to this conclusion it has been liberating. Discipline is no longer a chore but is a blessing. The last two days we have enjoyed a change in our son's personality; he's becoming a happy child. He's not done yet, but praise God for results. This time has brought us much closer as a family and the Lord is drawing us closer everyday. We feel it is very important to God and therefore to us that our family be in order. By God's grace and His love we'll continue to walk on that straight and narrow path. He is so good to us."

Children will learn as their parents are consistent that their obedience and attitudes are the parents' first priority. If mother is vacuuming or washing dishes and there is need for discipline, she should set the vacuum down and immediately administer the needed discipline—the dishes will wait while a child learns to obey.

Some parents will spank their children a couple of times for wrong attitudes or on certain occasions of disobedience, but then quit spanking if these areas are repeated. In such cases, the children win a battle of the will against their parents and will reinforce a child's attitude to have his or her own way. Parents must not lose that sort of contest: they must let their children know who is in authority. And consistency in spanking lets them know.

When our boy was about two years old, my wife spanked him for repeatedly disobeying her in a particular matter. Because she saw no clear change in his behavior, my wife remarked, "I think we might as well quit spanking him, and maybe it will just work itself out another way." My wife's friend heard her make this remark and wisely informed her that if she gave up now all the discipline to that point would be lost. And discipline in other areas would be weakened. So my wife determined to stick to the spanking no matter how long it might take until she saw a change in our son. The next spanking she gave to our son was the last one he needed for that particular offense. When she had been most ready to give up she was actually only one spanking away from victory.

Every parent should make a sign and post it in the home. It should read BE CONSISTENT! By consistency in disciplining children, parents show the highest form of love. Discipline does not put children in a straightjacket; rather it releases them from disobedience and attitudes that actually bind and hinder their well-being and personality development.

Danny, age four, asked his mother one day, "Why don't you spank us everytime we're naughty?" A child inwardly knows when he's done wrong and needs to be spanked. Even though they may not actually verbalize it as Danny did, they feel the need, and desire consistency.

Once a child has been trained, and through the consistent reinforcement of the rod has learned to be obedient and maintain a right attitude when he is young, as he grows older a parent will find just a brief word of reproof may be all that's needed in order for the child to correct his or her behavior. Proverbs 6:23 says, "For the commandment is a lamp; and the law is light; and reproofs of instruction are the way of life."

Excuses for Not Disciplining

1. "He is not old enough to understand."

If a child is old enough to know what the word "doggie" or "ice cream" or "bye-bye" means, then he is old enough to understand the word "no." I have heard parents boast about how smart their children are by saying, "He can wave bye-bye already," or "He can clap his hands pat-a-cake." But when it comes to disobedience and being a nuisance to other people, they say the child does not understand and therefore must be tolerated. But this is just an excuse not to discipline.

2. "Oh, he is so tired today. He is always naughty when tired."

This is a commonly heard excuse for disobedience. It is remarkable that two minutes before the child disobeyed he was not tired. But after disobeying, suddenly he is "so tired." Even though the child may be tired, a child can learn to control his behavior and attitude.

3. "It wasn't his fault."

Johnny wants to play with a ball that sister Suzie is playing with, for example. Johnny kicks and screams, whines and fusses, saying, "I want to play with the ball."

A parent might excuse this behavior, thinking, "If he had the ball, he wouldn't be angry. So, I'll ask Suzie to give the ball to him. Then he will be happy."

Such reasoning puts the fault for Johnny's obnoxious behavior, by implication, upon Suzie. If Suzie were not playing with the ball, Johnny would be good. But it is easy to see that it is Johnny's behavior which is wrong. And Johnny needs to be disciplined.

Another example would be the case where Johnny lies to his mother regularly. But mother blames Johnny's lying on Pete, with whom Johnny plays. Johnny learned to lie from Pete. Therefore it is not Johnny's fault.

Even though children are around others who may show poor behavior, parents still must require proper behavior from their children. The key principle is to discipline for wrong behavior. The establishment of blame or responsibility is always difficult. It is the behavior, however, which the parent must act to control.

4.   "He's this way because we are not home."

If you are visiting somewhere or on vacation, you must not blame the new setting for your child's disobedience and crankiness. The child must obey you wherever you are. YOU are the child's security; YOUR WORD is to be obeyed wherever you are, whether shopping, at the zoo, or even at grandmother's house.

5.   "Oh, he's just not feeling well. He's probably cutting a tooth."

Parents need to be sensitive to children's needs for proper rest and special care when they are not feeling well and should not be disciplined for being sick. But disobedience cannot be excused as "not feeling well." If a child is very sick, he will be too sick to be naughty. But if the child is just down with a cold or a new tooth, the word "no" still must mean "no," and "yes" must mean "yes."

6.   "Heredity"—"Oh, he's just like his uncle Jim. Jim has a real temper too."

The rod of correction will deal with any trait that is not proper, even though someone in the family may not have had the rod administered. It's probably too late for Uncle Jim. But you can be sure that it's not too late for your child.

7.   "He will outgrow it."

The child may outgrow the outward acts that are
disobedient. But he will not outgrow the attitudes associated
with that disobedience. When children start school, for
example, they soon learn that if they want to have friends
they must not pinch or hit other children. They learn to
conform outwardly to certain norms of behavior. But the
attitudes which were behind the pinching and hitting will
show themselves in other forms of aggressive behavior. And
early discipline by a parent will correct the sinful attitudes.

11

TEACHING

Love

"Now therefore hearken unto me, O ye children: for blessed are they that keep my ways. Hear instruction, and be wise, and refuse it not."
                    Proverbs 8:32,33

Example   Discipline

TEACHING

"When I call to remembrance the unfeigned faith that is in thee, which dwelt first in thy grandmother Lois, and thy mother Eunice; and I am persuaded that in thee also. . . . But continue thou in the things which thou hast learned and hast been assured of, knowing of whom thou hast learned them; and that from a child thou hast known the holy Scriptures, which are able to make thee wise unto salvation through faith which is in Christ Jesus." 2 Timothy 1:5, 2 Timothy 3:14,15

Parents are the best teachers that children can ever have. And the greatest thing that parents can teach their children is the Word of God. According to Paul in the verses quoted above, Timothy's strong spiritual life was not the result of his attendance at some outstanding religious institution or a dynamic Sunday School program, but the result of being grounded in the Scriptures at home, from his early childhood. What we teach our children is vital to their maturity, their character, and their total well-being.

Before a child starts school is the vital time for parental training at home. Parents, therefore, should have the greatest influence in setting the course and direction of their children's lives and helping form their character and personality. As children grow it is important that they are provided with the proper educational opportunities. But a public or private educational institution should not be looked upon as the vital source of education in a child's life. An educational institution outside the home, whether it is public and secular or private and Christian, should fulfill the role of reinforcing what children have learned at home. A parent may look to the institution to teach children in areas they themselves are not qualified to teach, such as algebra or chemistry. But the basic values and principles that pertain to life and godliness need to come from the parents. If parents allow the outside influence of television, magazines, movies, and the philosophy of others to be the chief source of instilling values and forming character in children, then the education they receive will not be the one they need.

At one time I was a Christian education director and I found that one of the greatest needs children had was for parents to teach them at home. A bigger Sunday School program, dynamic teachers, or a sophisticated curriculum could do very little without proper teaching at home. Yet many parents looked upon the Sunday School program as rescue work rather than as reinforcement ministry.

One day I went into a Sunday School class of fifth and sixth graders during the Christmas season and questioned the children about the meaning of Christmas. They could give me information about toys and tinsel, but none could say anything meaningful about the birth of Christ.

Parents Need to Teach God's Word, the Bible

There is an important connection between the teaching and application of the Word of God to our children and their growth in obedience and happiness. The relationship between the Word and a person's happiness is stated by Jesus in John 8:32: "Ye shall know the truth, and the truth shall make you free."

Knowing the truth is the greatest liberating force in anyone's life. Many, however, believe that freedom means being able to do what they want to do. But true freedom comes only from having the power to do what is *right* to do. As children are taught the truth of the Word, and as they respond to it, they will experience true liberation. They will be free of selfishness, guilt and bondage.

The relationship between the Word of God and obedience is made by Jesus when He said, "Therefore whosoever heareth these sayings of mine, and doeth them, I will liken him unto a wise man, which built his house upon a rock" (Matthew 7:24). As children are trained to obey parents, they are also being taught to obey God and His Word. For it is the Word that is the basis of obedience to parents. Obedience to parents beginning in early childhood serves as preparation for a life of obedience to God.

"The law of the Lord is perfect, converting the soul: the testimony of the Lord is sure, making wise the simple. The statutes of the Lord are right, rejoicing the heart: the commandment of the Lord is pure, enlightening the eyes. The fear of the Lord is clean, enduring forever: the judgments of the

Lord are true and righteous altogether. More to be desired are they than gold, yea, than much fine gold: sweeter also than honey and the honeycomb. Moreover by them is thy servant warned: and in keeping of them there is great reward" (Psalm 19:7-11).

In this one small portion of Scripture is stated the tremendous effects and benefits God's Word can have in our children's lives. The Word brings them to a place of personal salvation, of wisdom, of joy, of enlightenment, of purity. The Word is the greatest thing we can teach them. Parents must be convinced of this. Parents must place its value above material wealth and goods.

If our Bibles remain on the shelf collecting dust, children will not be convinced of the true value of Scripture. Jeremiah said, "Thy words were found and I did eat them; and thy word was unto me the joy and rejoicing of mine heart" (Jeremiah 15:16).

Teaching children the Word of God involves more than just getting a few facts stuffed into their heads. It means teaching them to receive it as food and nourishment. A hunger for the Word can be generated by our reverence for it. The hunger enters a child when he sees God's inspired Word held up as a source of great treasure and sustenance. "All Scripture is given by inspiration of God, and is profitable for doctrine, for reproof, for correction, for instruction in righteousness" (2 Timothy 3:16).

There are three ways the Word can be taught. Certainly the superficial way is to teach it as factual data. This is to emphasize how many books the Bible contains, how it is divided into sections, who wrote each book, and when and where the writers might have lived. The second way goes deeper. It is to teach information contained in the text: what God created on which day, the divine miracles through Moses, what Daniel did to be thrown into the lions' den, etc.

The third way, which is the deepest way to learn from the Word, teaches the spiritual truths and principles of God's kingdom that lie behind the stories. As children see and understand these underlying truths and principles of Scripture, they soon learn to apply the Word to their lives by faith and obedience. This makes the Word become food and nourishment.

In other words, children need to know that Daniel was thrown to the lions; but they also need to understand the importance of Daniel's obedience and how God honored that obedience. They need to learn about the miracles of Jesus; but they also need to know of the faith among the people that released those miracles. This is to say that children need the Word not only in their heads but in their hearts. It is good that children might win a Bible memorization contest in church. But it is far more important that they learn to walk the way of the Word in the world in which they live. As the Word of God becomes food and nourishment to children, parents will be training them to be strong in spirit. Jesus said, "The words that I speak unto you, they are spirit, and they are life" (John 6:63).

There is an old saying, "Many people miss heaven by 18 inches." Eighteen inches is the distance from the head to the heart. The Word within develops Christlike character and the wisdom to look at life from God's viewpoint. With the set of priorities and values gleaned from Scripture, children will know how to make proper decisions, how to judge the character of others, and how to order their own lives.

As parents establish a spiritual relationship with their children through the Word they will be involving themselves in an area that will last their entire lives. As children grow older and leave home, they become independent in so many ways. But one thing children need not leave is the spiritual fellowship and counsel of their parents, established at home. It is this spiritual tie, binding the heart in Christian love, that remains.

When to Teach

There are two different times when the Word can be taught to children. The first is in a structured time. It is a planned time, an organized time. Some refer to this time as family devotions. It is a set time when the entire family meets to share the Word together. There are many ways to use this time for teaching, sharing insights, and for prayer.

Whatever the method used to fill the organized, scheduled time, the important thing is that the family participates together in spiritual fellowship. Scripture can be read, principles can be discussed, problems shared, hymns, and choruses sung, and prayers offered. Specific times of memorization and meditation of Scripture should also be encouraged by parents. These structured, planned times are a very important part of family fellowship and discipline.

But another vital time for teaching children is non-structured time.

"And thou shalt teach them diligently unto thy
children, and shalt talk of them when thou sittest
in thine house, and when thou walkest by the way,
and when thou liest down, and when thou risest
up" (Deuteronomy 6:7).

"Whom shall he teach knowledge? and whom shall
he make to understand doctrine? them that are
weaned from the milk, and drawn from the breasts.
For precept must be upon precept, precept upon
precept; line upon line, line upon line; here a little,
and there a little" (Isaiah 28:9,10).

Before our first child began school I used to get annoyed if my wife was not spending a lot of structured time with our child teaching him God's Word. One day she managed to get me to see that she was spending a lot of time teaching our child; but it was not structured time. I realized that simply living provides the greatest occasion for learning.

When Jesus trained His disciples He did not rent an auditorium for three years and have them sit, hearing series of lectures. He taught them from life, about His kingdom, while they traveled from place to place, faced problems, and mingled with people.

In our home we came to discover that God's ways can be known through the occurrences of ordinary living. We did not try to cram a lot of lessons down our children's throats in as short a time as possible. Rather, little by little, line by line, thought by thought, truth by truth we shared with them our insights into God's ways as we played, worked, or traveled together. In these spontaneous, nonstructured settings some of the most meaningful scriptural lessons were communicated. Jesus' disciples learned about the depth and expanse of God's love as they walked on a hillside and observed the lilies of the field. They learned of God's great power when they came to Jesus for bread to feed a hungry multitude

One day when our children were older, we were riding together in the family car. One of the children saw something that made him curious about magic. He began to ask questions about it. That unplanned moment provided an opportunity to teach him what the Word says about magic, about witchcraft, and about the occult. And we talked about how God's power is greater than Satan's power.

Another time I was watching a television program with the children. In the program story a person prayed for help. But the message about prayer that the story gave was trivial and unscriptural. When the program was over, I used the story they had seen to teach my children something about the scriptural view of prayer. The television program provided the occasion to give the children some helpful instruction on prayer; and since the story interested them, the scriptural insights did too.

All parents will find these spontaneous occasions for

teaching children. A Christian parent must look for them, anticipate them, welcome them. A child's curiosity and interest peak their highest during these unexpected, pleasurable times. These are moments God uses to teach things that are meaningful for a lifetime.

Because this matter of teaching is so important, there should always be one parent at home whenever possible. If your child has a question or a problem and a parent is not there to help find the answer to solve the problem, the child will turn to someone or something else for help without the guarantee that what is deposited in the child at that moment was the right thing. The matter of both parents having jobs that take them away from the home, especially during the preschool years when so much of their children's character is formed, should be carefully weighed and prayed about. Other alternatives to the family's financial needs should be considered. A child needs a mother or father much more than he needs things. One sure thing parents must give to children is the time and attention they need. That time will always carry practical issues in which a parent's directions, answers, and guidance for daily living from God's Word can be imparted to a child.

As children learn the Word and its application to their lives, they will also discover the great and personal love God has for them. They will come to understand that Jesus died for them, that His death was for their sins, and that He lives for them to be their Lord and Friend. Parents need to point children to Jesus, to guide them into a real and living relationship with Him. This can happen at a very early age. Young children are very open and have no intellectual barriers that would prevent them from reaching a place of simple and uncomplicated trust. Jesus said, "Except you become as little children, ye shall not enter into the kingdom of heaven" (Matthew 18:3). The greatest privilege and joy a parent can have is to be able to teach a child about Jesus' great love and all He did and lead a child into a personal relationship to Him.

Both of our children came to know Jesus before they were four years old. I had the opportunity of seeing our son, Joey, come to know Jesus as he opened his heart to Him. My wife led our daughter, Lydia, to Him. She gave our daughter some simple instructions; Lydia prayed and opened her heart to Jesus; and after prayer our daughter literally leaped for joy. That joy has not stopped to this day.

Teach Them Character

Character is something that is learned and developed in a child's life. It is not a gift or a prize or something that comes from taking a pill or eating certain foods. Christlike character is taught. The Bible says, "God is working in us to will and to do of His good pleasure" (see Philippians 2:13).

One important area that children need to be taught for the development of character is how to work. Many people have not been taught the principles of dependability, carefulness and thoroughness that are part of being a good worker. A parent might not be able to teach a child the technical skill of a certain job, like carpentry for example, but a child can be taught to develop the character in his or her life that will make a good worker no matter what the job. Children need to start at an early age learning to pick up toys and clean their rooms. And they can learn how to fulfill other household responsibilities as they mature.

Learning how to work keeps children from slothfulness and the attitude that "the world owes me a living." Learning to work helps to develop a child's appreciation for what he has and who he is. It teaches him respect for his property and for the property of others. And children can discover work to be a blessing and a benefit to them. The development of Christlike character in children includes other practical matters such as proper manners, etiquette, politeness, hospitality, neatness, and generosity.

As children grow it will also become important for parents to teach them the why's behind the no's and house rules they have been given. The why of a house rule, or a no, is not the reason for a child's obedience. They do not need an explanation as a basis to obey your word. A child does not obey because something sounds reasonable. The importance of teaching the why is to supply your children with the basis of why a parent does what he does. This lays a foundation for them to begin to develop their own personal convictions on matters that will affect their choices and decisions throughout life. Teaching children the why gives them the wisdom behind the rules they are given. For an example, they will learn it's not just that they can't watch certain television programs, but why those programs are not good for them to watch. They will learn why certain words are not desirable, why certain attitudes and habit patterns should be avoided. Also, the why will help establish the absolutes of God's Word and help children to be discerning in not accepting everything society teaches or demands.

Our teaching will also include preparing them for the various stages of growth and development they will go through, including preparation for adolescence and adulthood. As a child grows he may ask simple questions about birth or his sex, such as "Mommy, where did I come from?" At these times it is important to answer the child truthfully. Give him just enough information to satsify his curiosity for that moment. This will lay a strong and solid base for teaching him later in more detail about human bodies and the process of reproduction and social responsibilities.

Remember that everything will not be taught or understood in a day or a week, or a month or a year. Repetition is required. For we learn line upon line, here a little and there a little, all through life.

12

PROVIDING THE PROPER EXAMPLE

Love

EXAMPLE	"Ye are the light of the world. . . . Let your light so shine before men, that they may see your good works, and glorify your Father which is in heaven." Matthew 5:14,16

Discipline

Teaching

I enjoy a testimony meeting in church as much as anyone does. It is good to hear people sharing what God does for them in their lives. I also enjoy a testimony service when people share the way their lives have been blessed and helped by others. Family members especially should have positive testimonies to share about those God has given them to live with.

God wants parents' lives to be the kind of example that

is consistent with what they profess. This does not mean parents must never make a mistake or they will be judged for hypocrisy by their children.

Hypocrisy is evident in parents' lives if they live by a double standard. Children will know if parents live one type of life in public and a different type of life at home.

Parents need to live a life of integrity and openness before their family. They need to admit any mistakes or failings if they occur. They need to apologize if they wrongfully offend their children, rather than ignoring a wrong or trying to justify it.

When parents walk in openness and humility before their children, they do not threaten their position or authority before the family. If anything, they establish it. "Before destruction the heart of man is haughty; and before honor is humility" (Proverbs 18:12). Through humility parents convey their desire to live before their children as God would have them to. Humility also reveals parents' complete dependence upon God's grace and power in their lives to fulfill this desire. Jesus said, "For without me ye can do nothing" (John 15:5).

Without the example of a life that walks out the things that are being taught in the home, children miss the greatest influence they need to encourage obedience and happiness in their lives. The right example creates hunger, desire, and hope in their hearts. The wrong example creates bitterness and resentment. Jesus provides the example of a life that pleases God. He revealed the Father, not only in what He said, but in what He did. And it is God's purpose to conform us to the image of His Son. "For whom he did foreknow, he also did predestinate to be conformed to the image of his Son, that he might be the firstborn among many brethren" (Romans 8:29).

And Paul states, "Be ye followers of me, even as I also am of Christ" (1 Corinthians 11:1). Paul was not afraid to have people examine his life to see if he exemplified what he taught. Too often people use the phrase, "Don't look to me, look to Jesus," as a way of justifying their inconsistencies.

"Those things, which ye have both learned, and received, and heard, and seen in me, do: and the God of peace shall be with you" (Philippians 4:9). If it is your desire to see your children have Jesus as the Lord of their lives, it must be clear to your children that He is truly the Lord of your life. They will need to see from the choices you make and the priorities you set that you count your relationship with Jesus Christ as the most important thing in your life. Parents cannot fool their children about this. And if you love the Lord, you won't have to keep telling them; they will know it.

A parent should not fear being an example to his children. There is no need to develop a "walking on eggshells" attitude around the home. Being an example is an invitation to be open and free with those you live with. Being a good example does not require frustration and strife in order to be spiritual. Parents should show that belonging to Jesus means the freeing of a personality, not a putting away of the personality into prison. An example should be one that convinces children that God loves and accepts them and desires to express Himself through the uniqueness of each personality.

I believe that as I am open in my relationship to God and to my family that my children will also be open to God and to me. My children will be able to see if I am comfortable living with Jesus. And they will learn that true spirituality does not mean walking around with stooped shoulders, wearing black clothes, and keeping a stern and solemn expression on the face, but rather walking and growing in God's love.

It is important that parents stand as good examples in matters of character and attitude also. There are many things

adults do that children can't do because of age limitations
and maturity. But an example in attitudes helps them prepare
for encountering situations later in life. For example, parents
want children to show proper respect for authority. Yet if
parents disregard posted laws such as "Do not litter" or if
they breeze through a stop sign or drive faster than the
posted speed limit, then parents are not setting examples that
demonstrate respect for authority.

Be a Source of Encouragement

"A man hath joy by the answer of his mouth: and a
word spoken in due season, how good is it!" (Proverbs
15:23). It is wonderful to be able to say the right thing at the
right time. People need encouragement. A compliment does
wonders to encourage anyone.

One day I went to the power company to pay my bill.
When I approached the woman working behind the counter I
said, "Thanks for the good service. Thanks for the terrific job
you're doing. I really appreciate your company."

The lady's face froze. "What did you say?" she said.

"I said, thanks for doing such a terrific job. I just want
you to know that I think my bill is really a bargain. Why,
when I think of the light I have to see with at night, the
refrigerator for my food, the entertainment I get from my
phonograph, and all the conveniences of washing and cooking
that electricity brings for what I have to pay each month, I
consider that a real bargain."

"You know," she said, "I can't think of the last time
someone came in here and said something nice. You've really
made my day!"

People are constantly bombarded with criticism and
negativism. Complaining has become a pastime for many
people. How refreshing it is to your family when you display
a grateful attitude and disposition around the house!

For example, after your children have raked the yard,

tell them that you appreciate the job they did. Use good manners with your children, saying "Please" and "Thank you." Learn to express through your words appreciation for things family members do to make life easier. Another way of expressing appreciation is by telling children such things as "I'm so thankful that you are a member of our family." Children learn by watching a parent. Many times parents make the comment "I wonder where my child learned that from?" The answer is that most often a child has learned it from his parents.

Show a Genuine Interest

A great part of a child's happiness comes from knowing that he pleases the ones he loves. One of the best ways of assuring a child he pleases you is by showing interest in the things that interest him. This means giving time and attention, to listen to what he says, and to watch what he does. It also means spending uninterrupted time with him.

I used to feel that I was something of a king and my home was my castle. I expected everybody to serve me. When I came home at night from work, instead of showing a genuine interest in what my wife did that day or what the kids did, I headed for my easy chair, got the evening paper, kicked off my shoes, and relaxed. I made it clear to everyone that I didn't want to be disturbed by the things they had to tell me or show me.

One day as I was about to head for my chair, I sensed God speak to me about my attitude. I saw that I was not the example He wanted me to be, because I was seeking my own interests above the interests of others in my family. I realized that I must give up the attitude of expecting others to cater to me. I discovered that my family needed my attention at that moment, far more than I needed a few minutes of privacy.

The interesting thing is that when I began to put into

practice my new discovery, my family developed a new responsiveness to me and to my needs. They learned by my example to be sensitive to the needs and interests of others.

Follow Through on What You Promise

"Neither shalt thou swear by thy head, because thou canst not make one hair white or black. But let your communication be, Yea, yea; Nay, nay; for whatsoever is more than these cometh of evil" (Matthew 5:36,37).

One of the most important things to do *in front of your children* is to be a person of your word. When you say you are going to do something, do it! When you say you are going to take the children somewhere, take them! The promises you make must never be lightly spoken. Your children need to know that they can depend upon what you say. If there are times when you have made a hasty promise that you cannot keep, go to your children and tell them and ask their forgiveness. They will understand, and it will not weaken their trust in your word. However, don't make the mistake of promising them something and then forgetting about it or planning to do something else that seems to be more convenient to you. Failure to keep your word can be a source of deep resentment within your children.

This principle of keeping your word also applies when you say "no" to something. Children don't always have to be promised a lot of things. They need to accept a "no" just as joyfully as a "yes." Saying "no" doesn't weaken a child's trust, but saying "no" and not meaning it does.

Another important way of creating trust is by speaking truthfully to children. Parents should never allow a fairy tale or a make-believe story to take the place of truth. Trust is one of the greatest elements that contribute to a child's happiness. As you help develop this trust, you will be the positive example they need for their adult years.

Parents should make it a practice of not leaving their

children without telling them where they are going and when they will return. This will create trust in children toward their parents. If a parent 'sneaks out' mistrust and a feeling of fear and insecurity can develop within children.

The importance of the parents' example in the lives of children is graphically illustrated in the following song:

> My child arrived just the other day
> He came to the world in the usual way
> But there were planes to catch
>   and bills to pay
> He learned to walk while I was away.
> And he was talkin' 'fore I knew it
> And as he grew he'd say,
> "I'm gonna be like you, Dad;
> You know, I'm gonna be like you."
>
> And the cat's in the cradle
> And the silver spoon
> Little boy blue and the man in the moon.
> "When you comin' home, Dad?"
> "I don't know when—but we'll get together then,
>   Son,
> You know, we'll have a good time then."
>
> My son turned ten just the other day.
> He said, "Thanks for the ball, Dad.
> Come on, let's play.
> Can you teach me to throw?"
> I said, "Not today, I got a lot to do."
> He said, "That's okay."
> And he walked away, but his smile never dimmed
> And he said, "I'm gonna be like him—yeah—you
>   know
> I'm gonna be like him."

And the cat's in the cradle
And the silver spoon
Little boy blue and the man in the moon.
"When you comin' home, Dad?"
"I don't know when—but we'll get together then,
     Son;
You know, we'll have a good time then."

Well, he came from college just the other day
So much like a man I just had to say,
"Son, I'm proud of you.
Can you sit for awhile?"
He shook his head and he said with a smile,
"What I'd really like, Dad, is to borrow the car
     keys
See you later—can I have them, please?"
"When you comin' home, Son?"
"I don't know when—but we'll get together then,
     Dad;
You know, we'll have a good time then."

I've long since retired and my son's moved
     away,
I called him up just the other day
I said, "I'd like to see you if you don't mind."
He said, "I'd love to, Dad, if I can find the time,
You see, my new job's a hassle and the kids have
     the flu
But it sure is nice talkin' to you, Dad;
It's sure nice talkin' to you."
And as I hung up the phone, it occurred to me
He's grown up just like me—my son was just like
     me.

There is a phrase that often comes up in Christian
conversation. It goes something like this: "That person is so

heavenly-minded that he is of no earthly good." The truth of the matter is, if people were truly heavenly-minded, they would be plenty of earthly good. The real problem is that people are generally too earthly-minded to be of any heavenly good.

When we take on the mind of Christ, we discover that He is very interested in the way we live our lives before others. As we read the books in the New Testament, such as Ephesians or Colossians, we learn that Christians have a spiritual heritage and victory in Christ. Then these books go on to show how that spiritual relationship is supposed to work out in everyday living. We discover that the life hid with Christ in God is very practical.

God cares about the way we live our lives before our families. We find even the smallest detail in our life is important to Him. As a younger Christian, I remember going through a period of about two years when God had to remind me not to throw paper on the ground without going back and picking it up and putting it in a trash can. I found that attention to this area of my life came because God loved me as well as those around me. God was not being mean or putting me into bondage when He kept reminding me about trash that needed proper disposal. He did it to help me develop a new dimension of concern for others. I found that as I responded to His reminders, other areas of my life began to become more orderly too. I had generally been a rather lazy and sloppy person. I was unconcerned about a lot of things I should have been concerned about. I was disorganized, a very poor steward of the things I owned. But as I began to give attention to little matters, like picking up pieces of discarded paper, I began also to straighten up my room, to organize my dresser, and to take better care of my possessions and the possessions of others. After this period of attention to little details, I discovered new habits had developed in my life. It became normal and spontaneous for me to be orderly and careful.

As you give yourself to God to be a Christian parent, you will find that there are many small, practical areas that are important to God—even though other people may not regard them as important. God will make you sensitive to some little areas, however. They may affect the way you dress, clean your house, keep your yard, prepare your meals, or service your car. But this area, whatever it is, will become an important part of developing you into a proper example to present to your children and fulfill through you His ultimate goal of conforming you to the image of His Son.

13

A WORD TO SINGLE PARENTS

"Not that we are sufficient of ourselves to think any thing of ourselves; but our sufficiency is of God." 2 Corinthians 3:5.

Although the material in this book is directed to married couples, the same principles for raising happy and obedient children apply to single parents. If you are a single parent, be encouraged. The special needs you have can be a positive force to draw you closer to God. You must look to God for help; and remember that He promises to supply your needs.

Trying to find complete self-sufficiency will be frustrating and sure defeat in parenting. God can be your strength, your wisdom, your protector, and your provider. He will also be to your children the missing parent they need. "When my mother and/or my father forsake me, then the Lord will take me up" (Psalm 27:10). God's grace and love can be revealed to your family in very special ways as you look to Him for His special provision.

14

A WORD TO LATE STARTERS

"I will restore to you the years that the locust hath eaten."
Joel 2:25

If you have older children that have not been trained according to the principles of God's Word, don't be discouraged. It is never too late to start. God's ministry is a ministry of restoration. He can take you from where you are and begin to restore to you the ground you have lost with your children.

Begin immediately to obey the Lord in those areas of your life that He shows you need correction. Tell your children about your commitment to follow Christ as parents. Let them know if you have definitely failed in the past as parents. Ask for their forgiveness, too.

Then trust the Lord for the wisdom and direction you will need. Some things will begin to change immediately. Other things will take time and may involve a lot of hard work and different ways of doing things. A tree that has been growing for a few years is harder to uproot than a seedling; nevertheless, it can be uprooted. God will be your strength as you work to change your family life. He never intended for you to do this job of parenting alone anyway. "When I am weak," Paul said, "then am I strong. For grace is made perfect in weakness" (see 2 Corinthians 12:9,10).

The important thing is to start today. When an airplane is heading toward a certain destination, it is vital that it stay on course. Wandering off course just a few degrees will alter the destination. As you are shown adjustments you must make as parents, obey. Do what God shows you. It will mean in the long run that your family will arrive at the desired destination. Trust God today for your life and for the lives of your children.

15

A WORD ABOUT THE
HOLY SPIRIT

"Not by might, not by power, but by my Spirit, saith the Lord." Zechariah 4:6

There is a great attack upon the family today. The enemies are many, including satanic opposition, godless philosophies, and materialistic pressures. The Bible tells us, "Except the Lord build the house, they labor in vain that build it" (Psalm 127:1). A truly successful family is one built upon the foundation of God's Word and daily dependence upon the power of God's Spirit to withstand and overcome these attacks.

Being the parents of happy and obedient children does not flow out of a special technique, but flows out of a relationship with God through His Son, Jesus Christ. It is impossible for us by our own strength and skills to be proper parents. But God enables us to do the things He has called us to do.

If after reading this book it is your desire to be the parent of happy and obedient children, and you have never known the joy of a personal relationship with God through Jesus Christ, now would be a wonderful time to begin. First of all you must repent of your sins and confess to God that you have fallen short of His glory by going your own way. "For all have sinned and come short of the glory of God" (Romans 3:23). Then by faith in the shed blood of Christ receive God's forgiveness. "If we confess our sins, he is faithful and just to forgive us our sins and cleanse us from all unrighteousness" (1 John 1:9). Open your heart to Jesus and receive Him by faith as your personal Lord and Savior. "But as many as received him, to them gave he power to become the sons of God, even to them that believe on his name" (John 1:12).

When you receive Christ as your Savior, the Bible tells you that you receive a spiritual birth. You are born again, spiritually. Christ's Spirit is joined to your spirit. "Now if any man have not the Spirit of Christ, he is none of his. . . . Ye have received the Spirit of adoption, whereby we say Abba, Father. The Spirit itself beareth witness with our spirit, that we are the children of God" (Romans 8:9,15,16).

The Holy Spirit has come to be your Comforter and your guide. He will teach you to be the kind of parent to your children that God is to His spiritual children. He will lead you in the direction your family needs to go. He will take the things of Christ and make them real to you.

If you are already in this relationship with God through Christ, but find yourself defeated as a parent, allow that defeat to throw you upon Christ and His Spirit for help. If you know defeat, then you already know that you cannot do the parenting job alone. The Bible says, "Be filled with the Spirit" (Ephesians 5:18). That means to accept the power of God and have that power work through you. Ask Him now to fill you with His Holy Spirit.

Not every family's needs will be exactly the same. We need the daily guidance of the Holy Spirit to know how to apply God's Word to meet the specific needs of each family. God's ways are perfect, and He gives you the Holy Spirit to lead you in that perfect way. As you follow Him you will see

the peaceable fruits of righteousness in your life and the lives
of those in your family.

If you have any questions about your personal relationship with God through Jesus Christ, or about your relationship with your children, please write:

ROY LESSIN c/o
PARENTS OF HAPPY AND OBEDIENT CHILDREN
    BOX 7491
VAN NUYS, CA 91409

Information on conducting a "Parents of Happy and
Obedient Children" Seminar in your area may be obtained by
writing to the same address as above.

About the Author

Roy Lessin

Graduate of Bethany Fellowship/Minneapolis, Minnesota

Ordained at the Bethany Church/Minneapolis, Minnesota

Director of Christian Education/Oakland, California

Missionary to Mexico and Puerto Rico

Presently vice-president of Outreach Publications

Staff writer of Dayspring Greeting Cards

Bible Teacher

Conductor of HOW TO BE THE PARENTS OF HAPPY, OBEDIENT CHILDREN seminar

Roy and his wife Charlene and their two children make their home in Glendora, California.